Chauncy Lively's Flybox

A Portfolio of Modern Trout Flies

CHAUNCY LIVELY

Stackpole Books

CHAUNCY LIVELY'S FLYBOX: A PORTFOLIO OF MODERN TROUT FLIES
Copyright © 1980 by Chauncy Lively

Published by
STACKPOLE BOOKS
Cameron and Kelker Streets
P.O. Box 1831
Harrisburg, Pa. 17105

Published simultaneously in Don Mills, Ontario, Canada
by Thomas Nelson & Sons, Ltd.

Cover photo by Sid Latham from Camera Afield.
Cover design by Tom Rowe.

Library of Congress Cataloging in Publication Data

Lively, Chauncy, 1919–
  Chauncy Lively's flybox.

  1. Flies, Artificial. 2. Fly tying. 3. Insects,
Aquatic. 4. Fly fishing. I. Title.
SH451.L56 1979   688.7'9   79-13407
ISBN 0-8117-2078-0

Printed in the U.S.A.

Contents

Preface

Few sports rival fly fishing in providing entrées into associated interests—allied hobbies which, taken singly, are absorbing in themselves. Leader-making, netcraft, rod-building, and general tackle-tinkering are all part and parcel of the flyfisher's world. Photography is a natural companion interest, not only as a means of recording the angler's catch, but also of capturing and preserving images of the priceless surroundings nature has provided trout. But of all the related avocations available to the fly fisherman, fly tying contributes most to his success on the stream and to the complete angling experience.

Fly tying has taken many new directions in recent years and it is an indication that fly dressers are seeking—and finding—original solutions to their problems. Practitioners who ply their craft on the food-rich, alkaline streams learn early that the wild trout of these waters are often selective to the extreme. Here, the traditional dry-fly patterns of the Catskills are giving way to new designs in which such considerations as correct wing silhouette, light pattern (the imprint made by the fly on the surface film), and floating posture are given high priority. Yet, compromises must be made to blend realism with practicality. Materials must be chosen that combine light weight with reasonable durability. The fly's design should ensure that it floats in approximately the same attitude as the living insect. These are typical problems of the fly tyer, but pleasant problems they are, for their solutions require a degree of experimentation that keeps the fishing alive and exciting.

I have tied flies for well over thirty years, and, coupled with its mother sport of fly fishing, it is nearly a way of life in our household. I derive much satisfaction from finding an innovative solution to a fly tying problem, then, taking it to the trout, discovering that it really works. Of course, there are times when the solution is found wanting and the problem still remains. Then it's back to the drawing board. Trout are the ultimate judges and they can at times be stern taskmasters.

This book presents a selection of fly patterns covering a broad spectrum both of use on the stream and methodology of construction. Of the forty patterns discussed I cannot claim credit for the origin of the Michigan Stone, nor of Hoagy's Little Orange Mayfly. The former was originated by Paul H. Young while the latter's origin is unknown to me, although it has been popularized by Hoagy B. Carmichael. The tying techniques illustrated are varied, to furnish the tyer with as many skills as possible, all of which are adaptable to other patterns. For example, the styles of detached bodies described for the Green Drake, Coffin Fly, and *Isonychia* Spinner may be applied to patterns representing any of the larger mayflies, provided the requirements of size and color are met. And the bunched, parachute hackle method of forming mayfly spinner wings is applicable to any spinner pattern.

The fly patterns offered here have given me many hours of enjoyment—both in tying and in use on trout water—and I am anxious to share these pleasures with others. If this book should stimulate the reader to experiment on his own and to evolve patterns distinctly *his*, then I shall be doubly pleased.

My grateful acknowledgment and thanks extend to James F. Yoder, editor of the *Pennsylvania Angler*, for kindly permitting the use of material in this book which had been previously published in the Pennsylvania Fish Commission's splendid angling magazine; to Alison Brown, Jerry Hoffnagle, and Neil McAleer for carefully steering a myopic author through the intricate maze of prepublication requirements; to Larry Rosiek, who lavished his usual meticulous care in processing the mountain of photographic prints; and finally, to my many friends and angling companions who have encouraged the assembling of these pages.

This collection of patterns was compiled and revised from columns that have appeared in the *Pennsylvania Angler*.

Nymphs

In the subaquatic world of the trout the stream bottom is his principal pantry. Burrowed in sand, silt and mud bars are the large mayfly nymphs of Ephemera, Hexagenia, Ephoron and Potomanthus, sharing habitat with dragonfly and damselfly nymphs. Under rocks in aerated riffles are stonefly nymphs alongside immature forms of the mayflies *Stenonema, Stenacron, Ephemerella, Epeorus, Isonychia, Paraleptophlebia* and others. Harbored in weedbeds of elodea and watercress are the little nymphs of *Tricorythodes* and *Baetis*. *Leptophlebia* nymphs are found in accumulations of decaying leaves and detritus in the stream's quieter stretches, as are cranefly larvae. The cases of caddisfly larvae cling to rocks and submerged logs while the nets of immature sedges are attached to the downstream sides of boulders or other sunken objects. When midge larvae and countless miscellaneous forms are added to the list it becomes apparent that the underwater food inventory is vast. In a healthy stream it is difficult to find areas devoid of bottom life. Small wonder, then, that the bulk of the trout's diet consists of subaquatic forms. It is all there for the taking and trout are extremely resourceful in finding their food.

While emergence of the winged aquatic insects is seasonal and relatively limited in time span, the larval or immature forms are always present in various stages of development within the trout's foraging range. Just prior to emergence many nymphs become extremely active. Species which emerge at the surface swim nervously about, occasionally rising to the surface and dropping back as if making a trial run of their emergence ascent. Those types that crawl out of the water to emerge migrate to shallow water while still others climb the stalks of water weeds. These are the times when artificial nymphs are most effective. The knowing angler watches for the signs: bulging trout taking emerging nymphs just under the surface; the writhing, nose-down attitude of trout feeding off the bottom; and trout holding in mid-water, moving their heads from side to side as they take drifting nymphs. There are also anglers who fish the nymph as a searching fly with deadly effect, casting a loose leader upstream and permitting the nymph to roll along the bottom with the current, past undercut banks or other obvious cover, ever watching for the telltale twitch at the end of the line which signifies the take. It's a subtle business, but effective.

The March Brown Nymph

Much can be learned about a trout stream by examining the extent of aquatic life on the stream bottom. Overturning a submerged rock or two—or scooping up a handful of gravel—will often indicate a stream's fertility by the quantity of nymphs found. On the other hand, the absence of nymphs means that the stream is probably polluted to a degree sufficient to eliminate the more delicate forms of aquatic fauna. A knowing fisherman will look for nymphs with obviously darkened wing cases, for these are the nymphs he can expect will soon be active and possibly emerge later in the day. Armed with this knowledge he can often predict the "hatch of the day" and make his choice of fly accordingly.

Among the more common mayfly nymphs inhabiting the riffly waters of many trout streams are those of the genera *Stenonema* and *Stenacron*, which include the familiar March Brown, Cahill and Gray Fox, and Ginger Quill. These nymphs are relatively broad and flat, designed by nature to be able to cling to the underside of

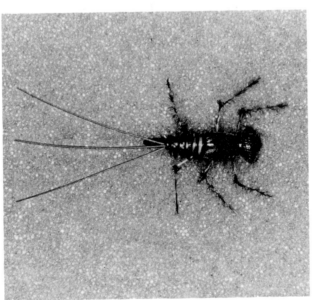

Completed March Brown Nymph

rocks in medium to fast current. They have characteristically broad heads, with eyes positioned on top, and rather large, barred legs.

The March Brown Nymph pattern shown in the photographic sequence is the result of a long evolution of subtle changes from the original condor quill pattern which we first described in the May 1953 issue of the *Pennsylvania Angler*. Some of the changes were made to improve durability, others, to enhance the likeness of the artificial to the natural. The pattern begins with a basic underbody, made by cementing a strip of heavy nylon monofilament to either side of the hook shank and tapering each toward the rear with a razor blade. This provides the required shape and flatness so characteristic of the natural and may be used as the basis for dressing any flat-bodied nymph. The nymph may be self-weighted by substituting strips of lead wire for the monofilament.

A single fibre from a dark condor quill (or, alternatively, from a dark brown dyed goose quill) is an ideal material for the nymph's abdomen. It is tough and self-segmenting, and the wispy flue on the edge of the fibre fairly represents the gill filaments of the natural nymph.

The big head, so prominent on the living nymph, is achieved by folding the quill extension of the wing case up and back, over a piece of chenille to give it depth.

Stripped hackle ribs are used for tails because of their extreme durability and because their natural curvature permits easy positioning on the hook. Care should be taken to avoid the use of ribs from large hackles for these are generally too clubby and stiff to be practical. Ribs from the smaller spade hackles are finely tapered and when soaked, in use, become soft and pliable.

Because of the general similarity of the March Brown Nymph to its smaller relatives, the pattern in size #14 is also effective when Cahills and Ginger Quills are prevalent. Like any representative nymph, it works best during the emergence period of the naturals and this generally falls between mid-May and early July, depending upon geographical location.

TYING THE MARCH BROWN NYMPH

1. Prepare a flat underbody by cementing a strip of heavy monofilament on each side of the shank of a size #12 hook. With a razor blade slice the nylon to a taper toward hook bend. Tie in brown nymph thread behind eye and spiral closely to rear of underbody. Half-hitch.

For tails strip the fibres from three small brown spade hackles. (These are located along the sides of the neck.) Tie in stripped hackle ribs at rear of underbody and spiral thread forward to midway point along hook. Trim off excess hackle ribs as shown.

2. Select a single dark condor quill fibre and bind tip end on hook with butt end extending over tails. Spiral thread over quill fibre back to base of tails and forward again to mid-hook. Saturate all thread on underbody with thin outdoor lacquer.

3. Attach hackle pliers to butt of condor quill and wind forward, being careful to avoid overlapping turns. Tie off butt of quill with two turns and half-hitch.

4. For wing case cut a section of dark gray goose quill slightly wider than body of nymph. Lay quill flat over body with shiny side down and tie in tip end over condor quill tie-off. With bodkin point spread a thin coat of vinyl cement on both sides of goose quill and trim away excess tip.

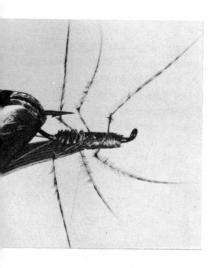

5. Invert hook in vise. For legs cut six fibres from a large, brownish wood duck flank feather. Tie a knot in each, near the middle of the fibre, forming a right angle as the knot is pulled tight. Bind legs in pairs to underside of body, as shown, and spiral thread back to edge of condor quill. Apply a small drop of lacquer to each leg knot.

6. Trim legs to proportions shown opposite. Apply a medium-heavy dubbing of tannish gray Cross Fox fur to about 2 inches of the tying thread and wind dubbing forward, taking care to avoid altering the position of the legs. Half-hitch thread behind eye.

7. Turn the nymph right-side up in the vise. Pull wing case over the back of the dubbed thorax and bind to hook with two turns behind eye.

8. Cut a 2-inch length of medium-diameter dark brown chenille and lay chenille over goose quill where quill was bound to fore end of hook. Hold chenille in position and bend goose quill up, back and over chenille. Bind down quill just behind chenille with two turns and half-hitch. Trim away excess quill close to windings. Cut off ends of chenille snug against each side of head and apply a drop of vinyl cement to ends of trimmed chenille to prevent unraveling. Move thread forward to eye of hook, whip finish and saturate finish windings with lacquer.

9

A Sulphur Nymph

If, as the old adage has it, a robin does not a spring make, then it is equally true that the emergence of a few mayfly duns doesn't necessarily guarantee dry fly fishing. Particularly in limestone streams rich in natural food, and especially during the early days of a hatch of typically long duration, the trout often pay scant attention to the initial appearance of duns. It is almost as if they must first acquire the *flavor* of the hatch, like learning to love olives, before turning their attentions *en masse* to the winged insects. On the other hand, the pre-emergence activity of the nymphs is a strong attraction to trout and they feed heavily on the larval forms at this time.

Much has been made of the importance of simulating the emerging nymph's ascent to the surface. Skues recognize this and Frank Sawyer, his modern-day counterpart, suggests that when a freely drifting nymph fails to interest a trout it should be activated by a subtle lift of the rod tip to represent the upward path of the naturals. Sawyer exploits this maneuver most successfully and every veteran nymph fisherman knows that the swing-around of the nymph, as the leader pulls taut at the end of a drift, is a critical moment.

On one of my favorite spots on a good sulphur hatch stream there is a narrow, deep channel bordered by grassy, undercut banks. At a bend there is a large mid-stream rock, over which the water flows and forms a curling eddy behind. Invariably a particularly fine trout occupies the choice position in front of the rock, often hanging just beneath the surface if he is watching for drifting duns; otherwise, holding deep near the stream bottom. I bent on a new Sulphur Nymph, soaked it in my mouth and crept through the tall weeds to a position below the rock. From my low vantage point I couldn't see the trout but guessed he was lying deep. A cast was made to a spot well above the rock and when I estimated the nymph was approaching the trout I lifted my rod tip to start the nymph upward. I had a brief glimpse of the trout as he turned to the left; then he disappeared in front of the rock. Reacting to the movement, I raised the rod and the trout was on—and solidly. With reel screeching and rod bowed, I scrambled to my feet and raced along the bank after him. He was a strong, heavy fish and in his upstream dash he ducked under the bank, scattering other trout helter-skelter. Where the water broadens upstream he made a wide circle, bolted downstream and I finally caught up with him just above a footbridge. There we had the final round and he came to net, one of the handsomest specimens of brown trout

I had ever seen. He was a tired warrior—and with good reason—for he had raced, upstream and down, nearly 100 yards. Gently I backed out the barbless hook of the nymph and lowered him into the water, holding him in the swimming position until he was able to operate under his own steam, whereupon he swam straightaway to the opposite bank and disappeared under the overhang.

The Sulphur Nymph is brownish with golden yellow and amber markings. The three tails are fronded and the legs are distinctly spreckled. The Sulphur Nymph pattern is dressed over a flat underbody formed by gluing .015-inch monofilament strips to the sides of the shank and tapering them with a razor blade at the rear. The mottled effect in the abdomen is achieved by winding a brown condor quill fibre over a previously wound cream ostrich herl. A brown-dyed goose quill fibre may be substituted for condor if the latter is not available.

The formed legs shown in the illustrations are optional and, if one is inclined toward stark simplicity, a throat of partridge fibres may be used instead. However, I'd like to urge you to at least give the formed legs a try because the method is uncomplicated and in use they lay back under the body with tarsi bent outward in convincing fashion.

The fur dubbing for the pattern's thorax is medium brown in shade and may be blended from any combination of furs and/or yarns plucked from the skein. Many fly tyers now mix dubbing in a kitchen blender (with milady's permission, of course) and material supply houses are beginning to stock premixed dubbing in virtually every shade, making the job of matching colors an easy one, indeed.

Completed Sulphur Nymph

TYING A SULPHUR NYMPH

1. Cut two .015-inch monofilament strips, slightly shorter than the shank of a size #16 regular or #14, 1X short hook. Glue strips to sides of shank and when dry, taper at rear with razor blade. Tie in brown thread at head and spiral back to bend, as shown. Half-hitch.

2. For tails, select three small light ginger hackles and strip away all barbules except at the tips. Tie in tails and take a turn or two of thread under base to separate. Place a small drop of cement on base of tails. Tie in one each brown condor quill fibre and cream ostrich herl by their tips over the tails windings. Wind thread forward to middle of shank.

3. Wind ostrich in slightly spaced turns to thorax position and tie off. Then wind condor quill between turns of ostrich. Tie off and trim excess of both strands. Trim off flue of the ostrich herl on top and bottom; trim to about 1/16 inch on sides.

4. (Bottom view) With bodkin point, separate two fibres of a large, brownish yellow wood duck breast feather. Cut fibres close to stem and stroke to hold together. Lay the double fibre across underside of hook and bind its middle at rear of thorax position with figure eight turns. Repeat for remaining legs, spacing as shown. With bodkin tip, coat legs with thin vinyl cement.

5. (Top view) Spin dubbing of medium brown fur on tying thread and build thorax. Half-hitch thread behind eye. Bend leg joints with tweezers before cement sets and trim to size. For wing case cut a section of dark turkey quill to cover thorax and coat outside with vinyl cement. Cut a notch in one end of wing case and bind opposite end behind eye.

6. Lift free end of wing case and coat underside with vinyl cement. Then press in place over thorax. Build a neat head, whip finish, and apply head lacquer.

The Dark *Isonychia* Nymph

Mayflies of the genus *Isonychia* are indigenous to most trout streams. Fishermen have dubbed them with such names as the Leadwing Coachman, White-Gloved Howdy, Slate Drake and others. Relatively large, handsome insects, these mayflies make their appearance mainly in June and July, when *I. bicolor* and *I. albomanicata* emerge. Particularly distinctive are the spinners of these two species, whose ruddy bodies seem to almost glow against the light of the setting sun. Lesser known is a very dark *Isonychia* with a nearly black body which emerges in late August and September.

The nymphs of *Isonychia*, like some of the larger stonefly nymphs, are known to occasionally indulge themselves in eating small larval forms, and both regularly emerge as winged adults after crawling out of the water on rocks or logs. But for dire emergencies nature seems to have provided *Isonychia* nymphs with a built-in optional method of emergence which I doubt stonefly nymphs have. At Penn's Creek we once had the rare experience of watching *I. bicolor* duns emerge *at the surface* in midstream. The big stream was in spate following a cloudburst and she was a raging torrent from bank to bank. Fast, high water covered boulders which were normally exposed and the *bicolor* nymphs, being strong swimmers, were able to reach the surface and emerge in the manner of most mayflies. It was an act of desperation, but a successful one, which stonefly nymphs could never have accomplished, for they are crawlers, not swimmers.

There are few mayflies which offer better opportunity for close observation of the emergence process than those of *Isonychia*. Late one August our family was camped at Poe Paddy, on the banks of Penn's Creek. When fishing became slow under the hot afternoon sun it was my custom to put aside my rod for an hour or two and explore the stream bottom for nymphs to photograph. One day I overturned a rock and found a fine specimen of a dark *Isonychia* nymph alongside a *perla* stonefly nymph. Both were carried to camp and placed separately in white paper plates filled with stream water. Several photographs were made of the *Isonychia* nymph and its plate was pushed aside while I concentrated on the other. As I rearranged my gear the *Isonychia* nymph began to tremble violently and it crawled up the side of the plate, halfway out of the water. Sensing that something was about to happen, I moved the plate back into position but I was too late. By the time I had refocused my camera the dark dun had already emerged and was standing beside the empty nymph case, drying his wings. Photographs of the nymph and freshly emerged dun are shown on this page.

The Dark *Isonychia* Nymph pattern is particularly effective in the fall. Since the natural nymphs concentrate in shallow water prior to emergence, the artificial should be fished in such places, particularly around exposed boulders. Caution should be taken, though, to cast softly and keep a low silhouette for trout are extra shy in shallow water.

Dark *Isonychia* nymph just prior to emergence

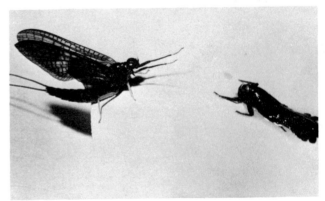

Freshly emerged dun and empty nymphal case

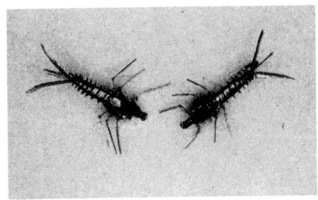

Completed Dark *Isonychia* Nymphs

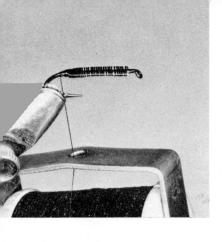

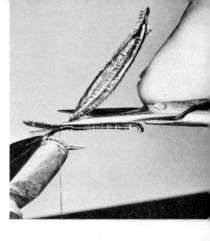

1. Prepare a flat underbody by cementing .020-inch monofilament strips to opposite sides of the shank of a size #12, long shank hook. Taper strips at rear. Tie in fine black thread behind eye and wrap closely to rear of underbody. Half-hitch.

2. For tails select three brownish-bronze peacock herls and tie in tips at rear of underbody. Trim off excess herls as shown.

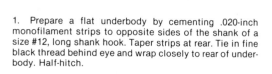

3. Select a single fibre from a condor wing quill, dyed black, and tie in by its tip over base of tails. (A black-dyed goose quill fibre may be substituted for condor.) Grip butt of quill fibre with hackle pliers and wind forward in close (but not overlapping) turns.

4. Tie off quill fibre, leaving enough space for short thorax behind eye.

5. For wing case cut a section of black-dyed duck or goose quill, slightly wider than the underbody, and tie in by tip at fore end of quill body.

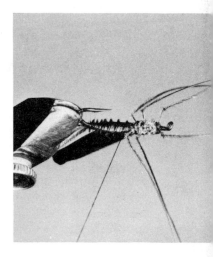

6. Invert hook in vise. For jointed legs, tie a simple knot in each of six dark gray goose quill fibres. Set legs in cement on underside of thorax. When cement has set wind thread crisscross over leg butts and half-hitch at rear of thorax position. Trim legs to desired size.

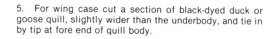

7. Return hook to upright position in vise. Wax a short length of the tying thread next to the hook and dub rather fully with black angora yarn, pulled from the skein. Wind dubbing forward without disturbing position of legs. Tie off behind eye.

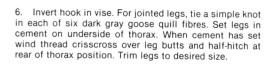

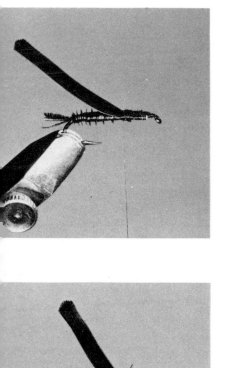

8. Pull wing case forward over thorax and tie off behind eye. Trim excess as shown. Then whip-finish thread and apply finish lacquer to head. Coat wing case with vinyl cement and apply a drop to leg joints.

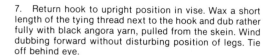

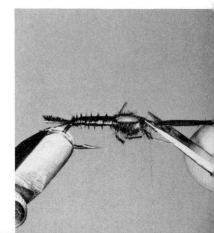

The *Paraleptophlebia* Nymph

Unlike the spectacular array of wildflowers in spring, the trout stream insects of the early season are mainly somber of dress. The little stoneflies and caddisflies of April are generally blackish to dirty gray and the best-known of the early mayflies—the Quill Gordons and Hendricksons—have drab, dun colored wings and brownish bodies. Overlapping these familiar hatches is another group of mayflies which, except for their diminutive size, roughly fit the description of the first two. Variously called Blue Duns, Slate-Winged Mahogany Duns, Early Blue Quills, or other descriptive names, the little mayflies of the genus *Paraleptophlebia* play an important role in the sequence of early hatches on many eastern streams. *P. adoptiva* is perhaps the best-known species of this genus east of the Mississippi River, enjoying wide distribution throughout the East and Midwest.

Most *Paraleptophlebia* nymphs are ¼ to ⅜ inch long and brown to brownish olive in coloration. They may be recognized by their deeply forked gills and the downward position of the mouth parts, somewhat like the head of a grasshopper. They move with a snakelike motion but are not especially adept as swimmers. They are primarily crawlers and are found not only in relatively slack water where detritus accumulates but in moving water over gravel bottom as well. Emergence takes place at the surface, and the nymphs often drift great distances before emergence is completed, making them readily available to trout.

Fur-bodied nymphs have been in widespread use for a long time, due largely to the versatility of fur as a fly-dressing medium. In recent years this popularity has been boosted even further by the introduction of the new synthetic fibers—the "poly-furs"—which may be used singly or in combination with natural furs to achieve virtually any color or texture desired. And although the synthetics are used extensively in dry flies, when they are unanointed with floatants they sink readily because they contain no natural oils. Armed with a modest supply of animal furs and dyed synthetics, the fly tyer is equipped to tackle any color-matching problem, particularly if he has access to a kitchen blender.

There is an interesting technique in fashioning fur bodies which lends itself perfectly to the dressing of small nymphs such as the *Paraleptophlebia* pattern illustrated here. Poul Jorgensen refers to it as "sculpturing in fur," and the first step is to form a fur chenille abdomen with the loop method of dubbing. Then the fur is trimmed rather close on top and bottom; finally, the sides are contoured to the desired taper. The result is a flat, tapered abdomen with a high degree of translucency. The thorax is made of fur dubbed conventionally on the waxed tying thread and wound to form an ovoid bulge in the forward half of the fly. A notched quill section is set in place to represent the wing case, and partridge or grouse hackle fibres serve as legs. The tails, which are bound in place before the body is formed, are three muskrat or mink guard hairs. The guard hairs of the water animals are extremely tough and resilient, making them ideal for tail material of great durability. The shortness of most guard hairs limits their use to relatively small flies but as tails for the *Paraleptophlebia* Nymph they are well-suited.

Since the naturals emerge at the surface in water of moderate flow, hooks of heavy wire are generally not required. However, the often swollen condition of the streams early in the season justifies carrying a few extra nymphs dressed on stouter wire, just in case.

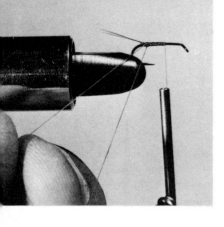

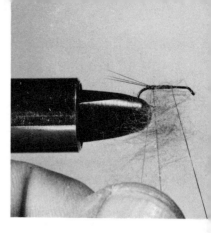

TYING THE *PARALEPTOPHLEBIA* NYMPH

1. Tie in fine, brown tying thread at bend of size #16 hook. For tails, select three brownish guard hairs of muskrat or mink and bind to shank at bend. Tails should be slightly longer than shank. Then form a 3-inch loop of the tying thread, as shown, and wind thread forward to about mid-shank.

2. Insert several tufts of reddish-brown fur in the loop and arrange uniformly between thread strands. Then bring strands together, closing loop and locking fur in place.

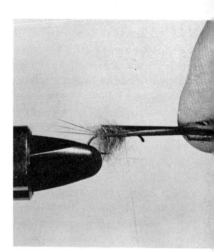

3. Clamp hackle pliers to end of closed loop and twirl pliers, twisting fur into a thick chenille.

4. Wind fur chenille forward, tie off at thorax position, and remove excess. Trim fur flat, above and below shank, then trim each side to a taper.

5. Wax an inch or so of the tying thread next to the hook and apply fur by rolling between fingertips. Wind dubbing to form thorax, as shown, and tie off behind eye.

6. Cut a section of duck quill dyed black, slightly wider than thorax. Cut a notch in one end of quill and bind in position as wing case. Apply vinyl cement to underside of wing case and press against top of thorax. Trim excess quill at eye.

7. For legs, tie in a few fibres of partridge or grouse hackle at throat. Then build a head of thread, whip finish, and apply head lacquer.

8. The finished *Paraleptophlebia* Nymph; it's easier tied then spelled.

A *Tricorythodes* Nymph

It seems a paradox that a genus of mayflies which has prevailed on earth for several millennia was only discovered by anglers as recently as a few decades ago. Yet, despite its abundance in many streams, the little two-winged *Tricorythodes* went unheralded except by entomologists until relatively recent years. Charlie Fox aptly called it one of the "hidden hatches" and it is true that unless one knows what to watch for its presence could go unnoticed.

Indeed, many a hapless angler has fished right through the hatch without suspecting that an emergence of duns or a fall of spinners was taking place, save for the frantic feeding activity of the trout. It may be that the tiny insects were formerly mistaken for midges—or perhaps anglers were loathe to believe that mayfly hatches could occur at such an early hour. For whatever reason the *Tricorythodes* was neglected in the earlier years, it is now recognized as one of the most fascinating hatches in all of fly fishing.

To think of the *Tricorythodes* as anything but a first-class dry fly insect would seem to be a sacrilege but there are times when its nymph warrants a representation, too. I first began experimenting with a tie for the nymph on a cold February evening quite a few years ago, and, like many patterns born of winter boredom, it remained unused in my box for several years. It finally had its baptism in 1968, on the South Branch of the Michigan Au Sable River, and the incident was an eye-opener.

Early one August morning I had gone with young Doug Slocum to a beautiful stretch in the Mason grant. We arrived at the river above a long bend as the *Tricorythodes* began to emerge. In the low, slanting rays of sunlight we could see many duns leave the water in char-

acteristic slow, vertical flight. Moreover, the trout were rising everywhere—not with the gentle rise forms usually associated with their feeding on small insects, but with slashing, noisy splashes that send one's adrenalin coursing.

Guessing that the hectic feeding was on emerging nymphs, I bent on one of the untried *Tricorythodes* nymphs and began fishing it across and down, allowing it to swing just under the surface. I don't mean to brag, but in the next hour or so *every* cast brought a hooked trout. Some were lost but many were landed and released and all in all, it was about the busiest fishing I had ever encountered.

I met Doug at the bend later and gave him one of the little nymphs, and he promptly began to emulate my performance. Then he disappeared behind the back-channel side of a small island and I soon heard an outburst of yelling and splashing. When I arrived on the scene Doug was reeling in an empty leader and muttering to himself. He had just lost, on 7X, the biggest brown trout he had ever hooked in daylight. There have been many pleasant experiences with the *Tricorythodes* Nymph in subsequent years but none could match that wild morning on the Au Sable.

The nymphs of *T. atratus* and *T. stygiatus*, the two predominant species in the East and Midwest, range in color from dark to light brown, and our pattern represents a compromise between the two extremes of color. The pattern is basically a Skues-type nymph and, because of its small size, no attempt has been made to simulate the flat abdomen of the natural, nor does this feature appear to be necessary. In the original pattern I used the tips of three pheasant fibres as tails and continued winding the same fibres to form the abdomen. However, the tails proved too fragile to be practical and muskrat guard hairs were substituted with excellent results. No problem of durability is presented in the use of pheasant tail fibres to form the abdomen, provided it is ribbed in the opposite direction with gold wire. Although a size #20 hook of 1X short shank is recommended, the nymph may also be dressed on a regular shank #20 by tying in the tails slightly ahead of the bend and dressing the body a little shorter than normal. The actual body length of the nymph, less tails, is about $3/16$ inch.

I'll have to admit that my favorite *Tricorythodes* fishing is to the fall of spinners, followed in preference by fishing to the duns on the surface. But when the trout ignore the duns for emerging nymphs I'm not one to disappoint them, and for those times the *Tricorythodes* Nymph has found a permanent place in my box.

Completed *Tricorythodes* Nymph

TYING A
TRICORYTHODES NYMPH

1. Clamp a size #20, 1X short shank hook in vise and bind fine, black thread to shank behind eye. Select eight brown fibres from a ring-neck pheasant tail feather and tie in behind eye with tips protruding in front by about the length of the shank. With fibres positioned on top of shank, wind thread halfway to bend. Then pull fibres upright and take a turn behind to secure.

2. Wind thread back to bend. For tails, select three brownish muskrat guard hairs and tie in at bend. Spread tails and make a turn of thread underneath and against base of tails. Tails should be slightly longer than shank.

3. Select two pheasant tail fibres and tie in, along with a 3-inch length of fine, gold wire, at bend. Then, with thread, build up a slightly tapered underbody. Wind thread forward to base of pheasant fibres at middle of shank.

4. Twist the two rearward fibres together and wind forward clockwise, to form abdomen. Tie off at middle of shank and trim excess.

5. Wind gold wire counterclockwise in spaced turns, as ribbing, and tie off. Cut or break off excess. Then wax about 1 inch of thread next to shank and apply dubbing of brown fur or synthetic. Wind dubbing forward to form thorax and tie off behind eye.

6. Split the pheasant fibres in front into two equal halves and press along sides to form legs. For wing case, pull vertical fibres forward and down over thorax. Tie off at head and trim excess, as shown. Then whip finish head and apply a drop of head lacquer.

17

The Snow Bank Nymphs

Dr. Paul Needham dubbed these small dark stoneflies "snow bank stoneflies" because they appear as early as February and may be seen scurrying along the snow-covered banks at streamside. Their appearance rarely coincides with stream conditions favorable for fishing the dry fly, and so fishing to the adult insect is not usually feasible. However, fishing a representation of the nymph offers good possibilities because trout feed heavily on the natural nymphs when they are available at the time of emergence.

The snow bank stoneflies belong to the genus *Taeniopteryx* and several species are represented, of which *T. nivalis* and *T. fasciata* are common in the rocky-bottom streams of the northeastern United States. The nymphs of these two species differ in size and coloration, the former being dark brown and the latter brownish yellow and smaller. Two artificial nymphs, representing the dark and light forms, cover the general requirements of the entire genus. Unlike most stonefly nymphs, which favor riffles and highly aerated sections of streams, the snow bank nymphs prefer the slower water of large pools. This is fortunate because in the usual high water of early season the trout choose to rest in quieter water, away from the rushing torrent, and they soon become acquainted with the little nymphs.

Although the snow bank nymphs are not as broadly flat as the nymphs of *perla* and *acroneuria*, they are nonetheless more flat than round. In our Dark Snow Bank Nymph pattern the flattish profile is accomplished by cementing two strips each of .012-inch (about six to eight pound test) monofilament to the two sides of the hook shank. The flat underbody thus provided influences the shape of the finished nymph, approximating the form of the natural.

The center rib of a hackle feather, stripped of its barbules, is an ideal material for the abdomen because it presents the effect of alternating light and dark bands. To avoid splitting, the rib should be first thoroughly soaked in water. For the utmost in durability it is advisable to thinly coat the underbody with cement and to wind the hackle rib over the cement before it hardens.

The legs of the nymph are made from strands of Nymo thread, bound to the underside of the thorax. I am indebted to Paul Antes, of Pittsburgh, for the following method, which works well with legs made of both Nymo and feather fibres.

First bind the legs to the underside of the thorax and trim them to finished length. Then touch a hot needle to the forward side of each leg at the joint position. This

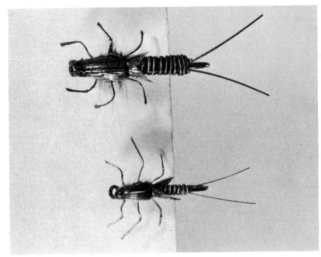

Top: Dark Snow Bank Nymph
Bottom: Light Snow Bank Nymph

places a permanent "set" in the leg material and forms a perfect joint which remains after repeated soakings. It's that simple. However, it's a good idea to first experiment with scrap material to determine just how hot the needle should be. In general, a red-hot needle is too hot and will burn through the material. Allowing the needle to cool a second or so is usually about right.

Alternatively, the legs may be fashioned of individual goose or duck quill fibres of appropriate color. Having bound the fibres in position, trim them to proper length and coat with thin acrylic lacquer or vinyl cement. After the coating has begun to set, use tweezers to bend the leg joints. Then allow the coating to cure thoroughly.

The dressing of the Light Snow Bank Nymph is similar to the procedure shown here, with the substitution of the following materials:

Hook: Size #16, heavy wire (strips of monofil cemented to sides)

Tying thread: Yellow

Tails: Two stripped ginger hackle ribs

Abdomen: Stripped medium ginger hackle rib, well soaked

Wing case: Section of gray mallard wing quill

Legs: Golden brown Nymo thread (or duck quill fibres)

Thorax: Dubbing of beaver fur mixed with yellow spun fur

TYING THE SNOW BANK NYMPH

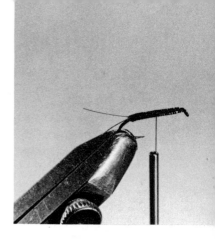

1. Place a size #14, heavy wire hook in vise and cement a strip of .012-inch monofilament to both sides of shank.

2. Bind black tying thread to hook behind eye and spiral over underbody to rear. For tails strip barbules from two small, dark brown hackles and tie in as shown.

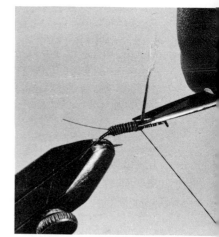

3. For abdomen tie in a stripped rib of a large, dark Rhode Island Red hackle, well-soaked. Spiral thread forward to center of shank.

4. Lightly coat underbody with cement and closely wind hackle rib forward. Tie off with three turns and half-hitch. Trim excess as shown.

5. For wing case cut a section of mallard wing feather, slightly wider than abdomen, and coat with vinyl cement. Cut a "V"-notch in thin end and bind over fore end of abdomen. Pull long end of wing case upward and half-hitch.

6. Invert hook in vise. For legs bind lengths of dark brown Nymo thread to underside of hook in thorax position.

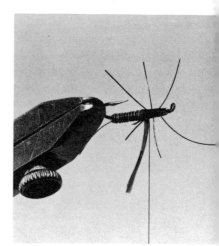

7. Apply a dubbing of dark brown Hudson seal fur to thread and wind thorax. Half-hitch behind eye. Trim legs to desired length and form joints by touching with a hot needle.

8. (Top view) Pull wing case over fur thorax and tie off behind eye. Trim excess and whip-finish thread. Apply cement to head and to tips of legs.

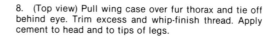

A Hendrickson Nymph

Few mayflies offer themselves to trout in such abundance and in so many ways as those of the genus *Ephemerella*. During a short period prior to emergence the nymphs nervously move about, sometimes rising toward the surface and settling again to the stream bottom, as if executing a rehearsal of their imminent entry into adulthood. During actual emergence certain nymphs rise to the surface, break through the film, and hang suspended with thorax exposed to the air while the thorax splits open and the winged dun emerges. The thorax is endowed with a waxy, water-repellent property called hydrofuge, which enables it to easily penetrate the powerful surface tension. Other times the duns emerge a few inches below the surface and ascend to penetrate the film. This they are able to do without getting wet because of a covering of minute hairs which traps a thin layer of air around the entire insect. Whichever the mode of emergence, the whole process, beginning when the nymph leaves the stream bottom and ending when the dun flies away to the streamside foliage, covers a span of several minutes. During this time the insect is completely at the mercy of the trout. The possibilities of deep-drifting nymphs, wet flies, emerging nymphs and dry flies are all presented to the angler.

The Hendrickson, *Ephemerella subvaria*, is among the most important mayflies in both the eastern and midwestern United States. The nymphs favor fast, well-aerated gravel riffles, and when a suitable habitat is provided they are generally present in great abundance. Entomologist Justin Leonard reported finding 1,277 nymphs of *E. invaria* and *E. subvaria* in a single square-foot bottom sample of gravel taken from the North Branch of the Au Sable River in Michigan.

Our Hendrickson Nymph pattern specifically represents the larval stage of *E. subvaria* but it is also appropriate as a representation of *E. invaria* and *E. rotunda* nymphs, which it closely resembles. The base color of the nymph is dark brown with amber markings, represented in the pattern by condor quill ribbed with an amber-dyed ostrich herl. Although not quite as durable, a substitute for condor quill may be found in the fibres of a brown-dyed goose quill feather, preferably those on the short side of the center rib. Ostrich herl is easily dyed with household dyes. The amber shade may be achieved by immersing a cream colored herl in a solution of five parts golden yellow and one part rust dye.

Because our streams are often swollen in early season when the Hendricksons appear, it is good practice to have some weighted nymphs on hand. The substitution of lead strips for monofilament in the body foundation provides just enough weight to carry the nymph down in the heavy flow without making casting an unpleasant chore.

The Hendrickson Nymph has become a favorite "searching" pattern of mine, and in appropriate water it has produced in almost every month of the season. It is often my first choice when trout are not showing.

Wild brown trout never come easy; at least I have never encountered a mentally retarded specimen! Recently, we had an opportunity to fish a beautiful stretch of water that harbors only wild browns and brooks. Since it was our first time in this water and trout were rising sparingly, I bent on a Hendrickson Nymph and fished it through the deep riffs and backwaters. The crimson-spotted browns it turned up were a source of great satisfaction. A perfect evening was capped by the capture of a heavy bodied beauty that took the nymph along an undercut bank. I released her with a reminder that I hoped to see her again—when the Hendricksons are hatching.

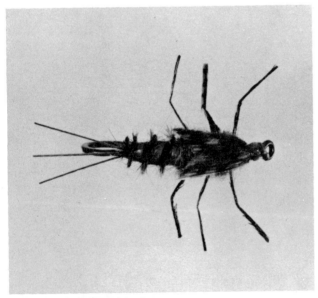

Completed Hendrickson Nymph

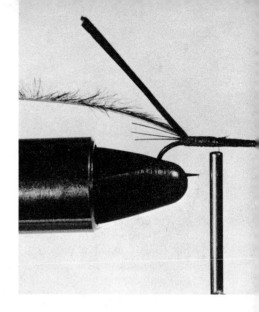

TYING A HENDRICKSON NYMPH

1.   Make a flat body foundation by cutting two strips of .020-inch monofilament (or lead wire if weighted nymph is desired) a little shorter than the shank of a size #12, 1X long hook. Cement a strip to each side of shank and when set, taper toward rear with razor blade. Then tie in brown nymph thread behind eye and wind back to bend. Coat windings with lacquer on top and bottom of foundation.

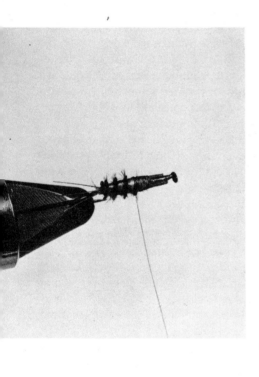

2.   For tails, strip barbules from three brown hackles and bind center ribs at bend. Tails should be about 2/3 shank length. Over tail windings tie in an amber-dyed ostrich herl and a brown condor quill fibre. Wind thread forward to midpoint of shank.

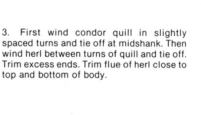

3.   First wind condor quill in slightly spaced turns and tie off at midshank. Then wind herl between turns of quill and tie off. Trim excess ends. Trim flue of herl close to top and bottom of body.

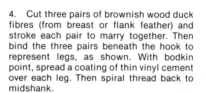

4.   Cut three pairs of brownish wood duck fibres (from breast or flank feather) and stroke each pair to marry together. Then bind the three pairs beneath the hook to represent legs, as shown. With bodkin point, spread a coating of thin vinyl cement over each leg. Then spiral thread back to midshank.

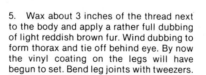

5.   Wax about 3 inches of the thread next to the body and apply a rather full dubbing of light reddish brown fur. Wind dubbing to form thorax and tie off behind eye. By now the vinyl coating on the legs will have begun to set. Bend leg joints with tweezers.

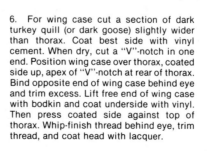

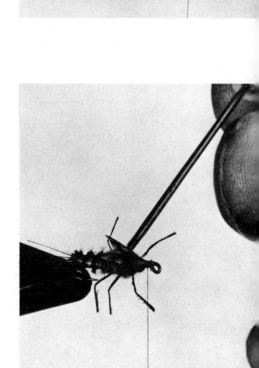

6.   For wing case cut a section of dark turkey quill (or dark goose) slightly wider than thorax. Coat best side with vinyl cement. When dry, cut a "V"-notch in one end. Position wing case over thorax, coated side up, apex of "V"-notch at rear of thorax. Bind opposite end of wing case behind eye and trim excess. Lift free end of wing case with bodkin and coat underside with vinyl. Then press coated side against top of thorax. Whip-finish thread behind eye, trim thread, and coat head with lacquer.

The Blackwing Nymph

Most fly fishermen carry artificial nymphs representing the larvae of mayflies, stoneflies, caddisflies, and less commonly, midges. One of the nymphs neglected by many anglers is the nymph of the damselfly, and it's one that can be extremely useful, both for trout and bass.

Like dragonflies, damselflies belong to the insect order Odonata. The adults of both are sometimes called "flying darning needles" because of an ancient myth that they sewed up the ears of truant schoolboys. Both are four-winged insects, the damselfly being the smaller and less speedy flier of the two. At rest the adult damselfly holds its wings together on edge over its back, while the dragonfly's wings are extended outward, as in flight position.

Damselfly nymphs are common in both streams and lakes, where they live in mud or detritus along the edges. They are great foragers and crawl haltingly along the bottom or through aquatic vegetation to prey on lesser insect larvae. They are slender in body and have three external leaflike gills at the posterior end of the abdomen. Full-grown damselfly nymphs are about an inch in length and generally dark olive, light olive, or gray.

One of the more familiar damselflies is the blackwing, of the genus *Agrion*. The common name of the adult blackwing comes from its smoky or rusty black wings and thin body of metallic blue or green. The Blackwing Nymph pattern is representative of several species of damselflies, and the pattern may be changed by varying the body coloration from dark to light.

Our pattern calls for external gills of grizzly hackle tips, tied in to the hook like tails. As most fly tyers know, good quality grizzly hackle is becoming difficult to come by these days. Paying for a choice grizzly neck is like a touch of high living. Being Scotch, both by nature and lineage, I've found the inexpensive cape of a Plymouth Rock hen to be perfectly satisfactory for any use, short of dry fly hackle, where grizzly is required. Thus, if I need two hackles for the wings of an Adams, or three for Blackwing Nymph gills, I don't have to deplete my limited supply of prime grizzly hackle.

The fur used for body dubbing is dark olive-brown, and the color is achieved by mixing two parts brown Hudson seal fur with one part olive angora yarn, plucked from the skein. Mix the dubbing to a uniform color with a dubbing needle or mix in a kitchen blender. Pretinted synthetic furs are also excellent, and if the appropriate shade is found, no mixing is necessary.

Damselfly nymphs have large heads and prominent eyes, represented in the Blackwing Nymph pattern by enclosing a piece of chenille in an extension of the wing case, a method used in the March Brown Nymph pattern previously described.

Damselfly nymphs are particularly effective in the weedy areas of the limestone streams. I've taken some fine trout in streams like Big Spring, fishing the nymph along the beds of elodea and watercress. In lakes, for bass and large panfish, I like to fish the Blackwing Nymph in the openings among the weed beds, allowing it to sink deep and retrieving it in short, slow strokes along the edges of the vegetation.

The nymph should be dressed on a 3X or 4X long hook. For bass I like a size #10; for trout a size #12 seems the better producer.

TYING THE BLACKWING NYMPH

1. Glue two short lengths of 20-pound nylon monofilament to opposite sides of the fore part of a size #10, 3X long hook. Monofilament should be roughly 1/3 length of hook shank. This forms the thorax platform. Then attach tying thread to hook behind eye and wind closely to bend. Half-hitch.

2. For posterior gills select three short grizzly hackle tips and tie in on edge at bend. Wind thread over hackle stems and spiral forward to thorax platform.

3. For ribbing tie in a 3-inch length of brown buttonhole twist (thread) behind thorax and wind tying thread over ribbing to base of gills at bend. Half-hitch. Trim off excess ribbing as shown.

4. Apply tacky wax to about 2 inches of tying thread. Sparsely apply a dubbing of mixed brown Hudson seal fur and olive angora yarn (see text) by rolling fur around thread between fingers.

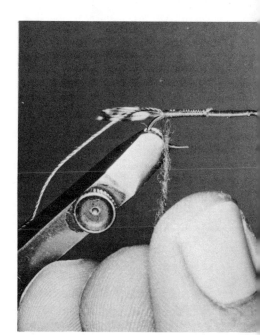

5. Wind dubbing forward to thorax platform and half-hitch. Now wind ribbing forward in spaced spirals in opposite (counterclockwise) direction. This prevents ribbing from burying itself in fur. Tie off ribbing where dubbing ends and half-hitch. Trim away excess end of ribbing.

6. For wing case cut a section of gray goose quill slightly wider than thorax platform. Bind thin end of quill to thorax, allowing butt end to extend over bend of hook. Coat both sides of quill with vinyl cement as shown.

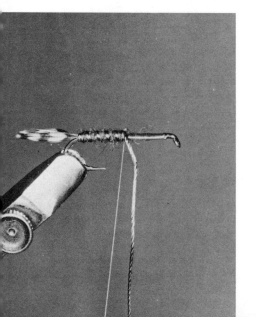

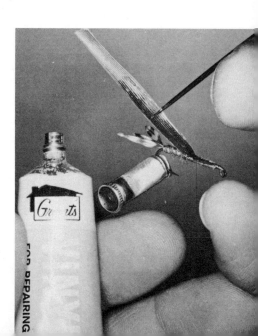

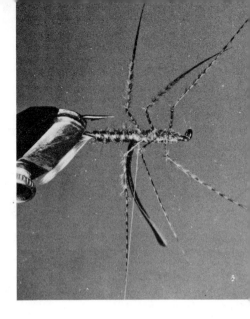

7. For legs cut six individual fibres from a large, brownish wood duck flank feather. Knot each fibre to represent leg joint.

8. Invert hook in vise and set the legs in quick-dry cement on the underside of the thorax platform. Wind tying thread over leg butts and half-hitch at rear of thorax.

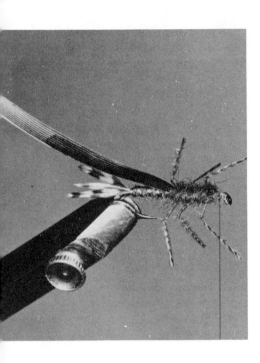

9. Release hook from vise and replace in normal position. Trim ends of legs to proper length. Again wax a short length of tying thread and dub with mixed fur as in photo 4. Wind dubbing over thorax platform, being careful to avoid moving position of legs. Half-hitch thread behind eye.

10. Pull quill wing case over top of thorax and bind down with two turns of thread behind eye. Half-hitch.

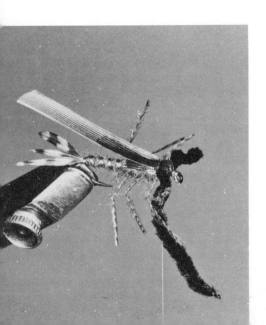

11. Lay a short length of medium-size black chenille over quill in front of thorax. Holding chenille in place, pull quill back over chenille and take two or three firm turns of thread over quill just behind head, as shown. Trim away excess quill close to windings. Trim chenille close to head to represent large, black eyes. Whip finish tying thread behind hook eye and cut thread. Apply a drop of cement to exposed windings and to each chenille eye.

12. Completed Blackwing Nymph.

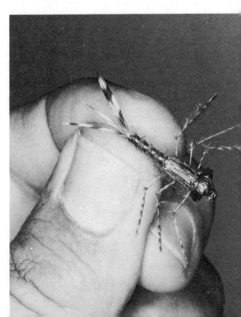

A Dragonfly Nymph

In the dim, underwater world of aquatic insect life the dragonfly nymph plays the bully. He sprawls in mud and detritus along the edges of ponds and streams, lying in wait for unsuspecting victims that he can catch and devour with surprising ease. His insatiable appetite fosters a diet of almost any living subaquatic organism, some nearly as large as he, and his own brothers and sisters are not excluded if he can catch them. He has even been known to catch and eat small fish. His weapon is an extensible lower lip, or labium, which he can whip out to grab prey as easily as a frog catches flies. When the labium is retracted it fits over the face of the nymph, appropriately like a bandit's mask.

Despite his clumsy appearance and normally slow gait, the dragonfly nymph is capable of fast pursuit of his prey for he has his own built-in jet propulsion mechanism. He breathes by drawing in and expelling water through a tracheal chamber at the posterior end of his abdomen, and by forcibly expelling jets of water he can move at a good clip.

Like the nymphs of stoneflies, dragonfly nymphs crawl out of the water to emerge. In lakes and ponds they climb up the stems of reeds and other aquatic vegetation to find their way to the air. It is during this pre-emergence excursion that bass pick them off easily.

I have been tying and fishing artificial dragonfly nymphs for a number of years and with them I have caught a wide variety of gamefish. Tied on long-shanked hooks in sizes #8 to #12, the pattern has frequently been an ace in the hole, particularly when conditions have been less than ideal. On lakes, during blistering hot weather when the bass were down, I've used the big nymph with success by casting it to openings among the weed beds and allowing it to sink deep. Sometimes it is taken as it sinks, at other times as it is being retrieved haltingly along the weeds. On trout streams I use the pattern when the water is too high and cold for dry fly fishing or after a freshet, when the water begins to become turbid.

Early one August morning I was having a delightful time fishing to midging trout on Penn's Creek when the skies literally opened and I found myself in a drenching downpour. The trout stopped their surface feeding, and soon the stream began to take on a milky hue. Hoping to get in a few more casts before muddy water made fly fishing impossible, I broke off my fine tippet and tied on a dark Dragonfly Nymph. Standing in the shallow

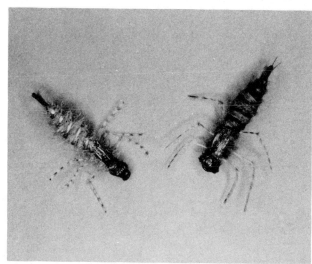

Light and Dark Dragonfly Nymphs

side of the stream, I cast the nymph repeatedly to the fast current at the head of the pool and allowed it to drift through a deep, boulder-strewn run. Once, as the nymph began to swing around at the end of a drift, a heavy brown darted out from under a flat rock and chased it a full ten feet before he took it with a mighty swirl in water so shallow it barely covered his back.

Dragonfly nymphs are heavily built, clubby creatures, and the essence of our pattern is its underbody, which determines the shape of the finished nymph. The underbody, shown in the first photograph, is cut to shape from thin sheet copper or aluminum and attached underneath the shank of the hook. It's a good idea to make a cardboard pattern of the underbody, from which the outline is traced onto the metal sheet. In this way you can make two or two dozen nymphs of uniform size and shape. Use an old pair of scissors to cut the metal sheet; tin shears will do, too, but they're a bit unwieldy for the delicate curves.

Our present Dragonfly Nymph is an improved version of an original pattern we called Old Ugly and described in the *Pennsylvania Angler* in 1962. Old Ugly's looks haven't improved a bit over the years, but the fish still find him a fascinating meal. Both a light and dark pattern are useful; both are tied identically except that the light version has a body of coarse yellow fur, ribbed with yellow buttonhole twist.

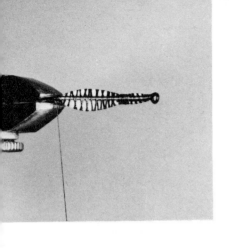

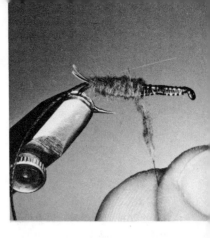

TYING A DRAGONFLY NYMPH

1.   (Top view) Cut an underbody from thin sheet copper or aluminum, of shape shown, and cement it to underside of a 4X long hook, size #8, #10, or #12. Tie in size A Nymo thread behind eye and wind to bend. Half-hitch.

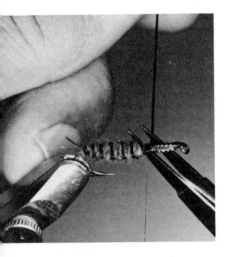

2.   Tie in two short, gray duck quill fibres in tail position to represent external gills. For body ribbing tie in a 5-inch length of black or dark gray buttonhole twist. Wax tying thread and apply heavy dubbing of dark mole fur by rolling fur around thread between finger tips. Wind dubbed thread forward and half-hitch at narrow thorax.

3.   Wind ribbing counterclockwise in spaced turns over body dubbing. Tie off ribbing and trim excess as shown.

4.   For wing case cut a section of gray goose quill, slightly wider than thorax, and bind tip to underbody at base of dubbing with glossy side of quill facing down. Coat dull side of quill with vinyl cement as shown.

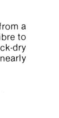

5.   Invert hook in vise. For legs cut six long fibres from a large, dark wood duck flank feather and knot each fibre to form leg joints. Coat underside of thorax with quick-dry cement. Set legs in cement and when cement is nearly set, wind thread crisscross over base of legs.

6.   Return hook to normal position in vise. Trim legs to proper size. Apply more mole fur to thread and wind forward to eye.

7.   Pull quill wing case forward over dubbed thorax and bind to hook behind eye. Half-hitch.

8.   Place a 3-inch strand of medium black chenille over quill behind eye. Holding chenille firmly in position with right hand, with left hand pull quill section up and over chenille. Bind down quill behind chenille with two turns and half-hitch. Then move thread forward under head and whip-finish behind eye of hook. Trim off quill section behind windings and trim chenille close to sides to represent eyes. Coat top of wing case with vinyl cement and apply a drop to each leg joint and to eyes. A drop of cement on whip finish completes nymph.

Mayfly Duns and Spinners

Much of the romance of fly fishing has been inspired by the Ephemeroptera, the incredibly delicate and beautiful mayflies, and rightly so. Even if they weren't a factor in fly fishing, and thankfully they are, I think I would still get a thrill watching the processions of little sail-wings float serenely with the current, and, lifting off, fly upwards to the streamside foliage. But trout do love them and so do birds.

I always marvel at how accurately swallows can predict a mayfly hatch, always appearing shortly before the hatch is to begin, lined up nearly shoulder to shoulder, perched on power lines near the stream. One warm evening in May we were lazing on the streambank in one of Falling Spring's upper meadows, awaiting the sulphur hatch, when several cedar waxwings flew to a branch overhanging the stream and began their own vigil. Once the duns began to appear on the water we became so entertained by the antics of the birds that we nearly forgot our reason for being there. They capture flying insects with a showmanship unmatched by other birds, changing directions in mid-air in a curious, sideways cartwheeling maneuver with tail feathers flared like Victorian fans. It's fortunate that nature provides a bounty of mayflies; otherwise, few would survive both trout and birds to perpetuate their kind.

Fishing to mayfly duns and spinners means fishing mainly dry flies and this, to me, is the most pleasant of all fly fishing modes. From the delicate placement of the fly to the deliberate but gentle reaction to set the hook, the aesthetics are of the highest order. Watching one's fly float uninhibited over intricate currents is satisfying in itself, but when a pointed snout parts the surface to engulf the fly and a surge is felt through arched bamboo, the ultimate has been achieved. Whatever else happens is secondary to that supreme moment.

Astute observers note that mayfly duns generally float with wings aloft in a single, vertical plane. In the dun patterns illustrated here the wings are separated at a modest angle as a concession to a principle of aeronautics. Every youngster who builds and flies model airplanes knows this angular arrangement as a dihedral angle which lends stability in flight, although in aircraft the angle above or below horizontal is relatively slight. In dry flies with wings as large as those of the natural insects this angular separation is necessary to ensure that they alight upright when cast. Similarly, a slight dihedral angle in the wings of spent spinner patterns is beneficial.

The tall-wing dun patterns should never be crammed into typical flybox compartments because the wings will eventually become warped and misshapen. I use compartmentless plastic boxes deep enough to accommodate my largest duns and lined, both lid and bottom, with a $\frac{1}{8}$-inch foam plastic sheet. Notion departments of variety stores carry the latter material under the trade name of Art Foam. This material is easily cemented to the plastic box with either rubber cement or plastic solvent. The flies are then lightly hooked in the foam in erect position, duns on the bottom and spinners in the lid. Thus arranged, no fly touches another and they always remain fresh.

Sulphur Duns

It is often difficult, if not impossible, to accurately judge the coloration of insects from their appearance in flight. This is particularly true of certain mayflies. In flight the beating wings often reflect the body coloration. The yellow-bodied *Ephemerella* mayfly duns—the several species which anglers have labeled sulphurs—are guilty of this visual deception. When the sulphur is on the water or in the air the overall impression is that of a yellowish insect, yet when one of the duns is examined in the hand the wings invariably are a darker gray. Needless to say, the angler who selects his artificial to match a visual image of the airborne insect is apt to be in error in his choice of fly. The obvious remedy is cultivating the habit of catching and observing the insect at close hand. A small aquarium net and a miniature folding magnifier add little weight and bulk to the angler's gear but are important aids in the capture and examination of insects.

The famous Sulphur of southcentral Pennsylvania must be classified as among the very best of hatches. There it first makes its appearance early in May, and the peak of emergence occurs around Memorial Day. From beginning to end it offers about six weeks of good dry fly fishing; there aren't many hatches that can boast emergence of such duration. On the water the dun is calm and serene, riding the currents for long distances before taking flight. Trout thus become well-acquainted with the naturals and often acquire a selectivity in feeding that places the most exacting demands on the artificial.

The Sulphur Dun pattern is the result of much experimentation over the past few years, and the general design is applicable to any mayfly representation of medium to small size. Use of the tall, broad wings of

Female dun of the *Ephemerella dorothea*

mallard flight quill sections is made feasible by coating the inside surfaces of the wings, after they are in position, with the thinnest film of vinyl cement. Not only does the liquid vinyl assist in maintaining the shape and flexibility of the wings, but it also helps to hold the fragile fibres together during hard use. The tips of the wings may be trimmed round or left pointed, at the tyer's option, but in either event the wings should be set straight on the hook to prevent leader twist.

The open palmer hackling sequence, running from front to rear, is a bit of unorthodoxy for a definite purpose. Here the intention is to flare the hackle slightly forward in front, and rearward at the tie-off in back. When the "V" is trimmed from the underside of the hackle the supporting barbules are set in the posture of the legs of the natural insect. The artificial balances beautifully on the water without tail support. Making the final tie-off and whip-finish underneath the base of the tails requires a little thought but if you can perform a whip-finish without a tool at the head of a fly you can do it equally well at the rear. Simply bear in mind that the whipping loop is passed over and around the entire fly as the finishing winds are made.

The male dun of the Sulphur is sufficiently different in coloration from the female to warrant a separate representation, although the difference need only be shown in the thorax. In the male version, in step 4, a short length of rusty orange-brown dubbing is applied to the thread. In step 5 the rusty thorax is wound from the eye to behind the wings. Then yellow dubbing is applied to the thread and the abdomen is formed as shown.

Left: Female Sulphur Dun
Right: Male Sulphur Dun

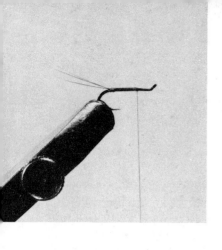

TYING A SULPHUR DUN

1. Clamp a #16 dry fly hook in vise and tie in fine yellow thread at bend. Select three cream hackle barbules and tie in as tails. Wind thread over tail butts and half-hitch about 1/3 shank length behind eye.

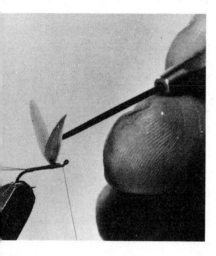

2. From a right and left gray mallard flight feather cut matching quill sections for wings. Tips of wings may be trimmed round (as shown) or left untrimmed. Match wings and tie to hook wet fly style with glazed sides of quill sections back to back. Effective wing height should be equal to entire length of hook, including eye and bend.

3. Pull wings upright and wind behind base to lock in position. Trim away butts and wind thread to eye. Then with bodkin point apply small drop vinyl cement (or vinyl floor coating) to base of wings and spread quickly to tips, removing any excess.

4. Select one each dark honey and pale dun hackles with stiff barbules as long as about twice the gap of hook. Strip away soft barbules near base and place hackles together with dun hackle at right. Tie in both hackles together by their butts in front of wings. Hackles should be positioned on edge, with glossy sides facing bend. Then wax about 2 inches of the tying thread and apply a dubbing of strong yellow kapok or spun angora fur.

5. Wind dubbing in a neatly tapered form back to bend. Half-hitch thread, allowing a little space between end of dubbing and base of tails.

6. Wind hackles individually in open palmer style back to bend and tie off each in front of tails.

7. Whip finish thread underneath tails around bend of hook. Trim excess thread and apply finish lacquer to exposed windings in rear.

8. (Front view) With sharp scissors carefully trim away a "V" from the bottom of the hackle, from front to rear.

29

The March Brown Dun

In the lexicon of the fly fisher, the March Brown is a familiar name. To English anglers it is the centuries-old designation of the mayfly, *Rhithrogena haarupi*, a large fly of the British Isles with mottled wings and a brown, banded body. Around the turn of the century, after news of the British dry fly revolution had reached our shores, English flies were imported in great quantity for American anglers anxious to try the new sport. With the entomological differences on opposite sides of the Atlantic it was inevitable that many of the English pattern would fail on our waters. A few bore enough resemblance to specific insects to warrant assigning English names to flies of our streams. Not the least of these was the March Brown, the borrowed name given to our *Stenonema vicarium*, the big mayfly which precedes the Green Drake on many streams in the eastern United States.

Although there is a superficial resemblance between *R. haarupi* and *S. vicarium*, the English fly is darker in body and leg coloration, rendering the British artificial ineffective in representing the American March Brown.

On waters where *S. vicarium* is plentiful, the hatch is often nearly as dramatic as that of the Green Drake. The flies are large enough to be attractive to above-average trout and the duns seem to have particular difficulty in detaching themselves from their nymphal shucks. They ride the surface for considerable distances and, once airborne, are not the most accomplished flyers for they often drop to the water time and again before reaching their streamside shelter. This prolonged exposure permits the closest observation by trout and a convincing artificial is in order if the angler is to be successful.

The March Brown Dun pattern follows the clipped palmer style of hackling, and the hackle is wound from front to rear, giving the fly maximum support on the surface film. Since the fly balances properly without requiring tail support, the tails may be angled upward in the posture of the natural insect. This not only prevents a distortion of the light pattern but permits the use of materials, such as wood duck fibres, which would normally be impractical as tails on the conventional style of dry fly. The body dubbing may be any fawn-colored or tan fur such as Australian Opossum, Cross Fox, or any combination of furs or synthetics to produce a shade slightly darker than cream and lighter than brown.

The wings of *Stenonema vicarium* are strongly prominent. They are represented in our pattern by the small, mottled feathers found on the back of a ring-necked pheasant, cut to shape. Shaping may be accomplished by several methods, such as the use of curved scissors or a special tool like the Wing Cutter, available from E. Hille of Williamsport, Pennsylvania. To me, the cleverest method of cutting wings of hackle or body feathers is one devised by Poul Jorgensen, the great Maryland fly dresser who has set a new high standard of excellence in his profession. Mr. Jorgensen utilizes a large toenail clipper, the folding handle type available in drug stores, and trims the wings separately. It is a surprisingly fast and simple trick which produces cleanly contoured wings of convincing shape. Naturally, flat wings of the required height and breadth must be set straight or they will cause the leader to twist in casting. However, with a little care this is easily accomplished and once set, a spot of hard-drying cement (Duco, Ambroid, etc.) at the base of the wings will keep them properly set indefinitely.

The March Brown Dun was originally intended as a "match the hatch" pattern but it has proved its worth as a utility fly as well. It has become my favorite fish finder on those occasions when the mountain streams are high and the trout are not showing, replacing the spiders I once used for that purpose. It seems to have the ability to draw trout—often above average in size—to the surface in heavy runs. Admittedly, "pounding them up" is not as much fun as fishing the rise, but everyone knows there are times when it's necessary. The March Brown Dun has come through admirably for me on many such occasions, and I hope it does the same for you.

Completed March Brown Dun

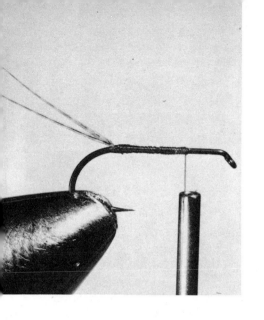

TYING THE MARCH BROWN DUN

1. Select a size #12 fine wire dry fly hook and bind fine, brown tying thread, such as Danville prewaxed nylon, to the shank near the bend. For tails, tie in two fibres from a wood duck flank feather. Take an extra turn or two of thread snugly behind the tails to separate them. Place a small drop of head lacquer on apex of tails. Spiral thread forward 2/3 the length of shank and half-hitch.

2. For wings, take two small, mottled back feathers of a ring-necked pheasant and cut to shape shown. (See text.) Effective wing height should be equivalent to overall length of hook, including eye and bend. Holding matched wings back to back, bend stems forward at right angle with tweezers. Leave a small space between bottom feather fibres and bend.

3. Hold wings upright over hook and set bent stems flat on shank in position. Bind with several turns and check angle of wings for straightness. Then take a few turns around upright stems at base and make corrections as necessary. Half-hitch around shank and apply a drop of hard-drying cement on wing base. Select a grizzly and a brown hackle with barbule length about twice hook gap. Strip off lower webby barbs. Hold hackles together with glossy sides toward bend and with figure-eight turns, bind them at right angles and on edge in front of wings. Bend stems forward and bind along shank. Trim excess.

4. Apply fawn-colored fur dubbing to tying thread and wrap a tapered body back to a point just ahead of bend. Half-hitch.

5. Wind the two hackles separately, taking a full turn in front of the wings and in spaced turns back to rear of body. Tie off, half-hitch, and trim excess hackle tips. Then whip finish or apply several half-hitches under base of tails. Trim excess thread and apply head lacquer to finish windings.

6. (Front view) With fine-pointed scissors trim a wide "V" from the hackle close to the underside of the body.

31

A Palmer Cahill Dun

Traditionally, the common names of anglers' flies have been assigned to the insects the artificial flies were intended to represent. Everyone knows, at least among angling circles, that *Ephemerella guttulata* is really the Green Drake, *Stenonema vicarium* the March Brown, and *Ephemerella dorothea* the Sulphur. This kind of descriptive designation has been used by fishermen since Dame Juliana Berners listed her twelve flies *"wyth whych ye shall angle,"* almost five centuries ago. But we now have a problem with a fly that has become a household name in angling. The Cahill, well-known to fly fishermen everywhere, is a fly used to represent some of the light-colored *Stenonema* mayflies and the name has been attached to the hatches themselves. Preston Jennings and other angler-authors have referred interchangeably to both *Stenonema canadense* and *S. ithaca* as the Cahills, noting that the differences in the two insects are so slight that a single pattern serves equally for both. However, entomologists have effected several taxonomic changes since Dr. Needham's *The Biology of Mayflies* was published in 1935. Dr. Edmunds (*Mayflies of North and Central America*, published 1976) has split the genus *Stenonema* and moved some of the species, including *S. canadense*, to a new genus, *Stenacron*. Thus, the Cahill twins have been separated and we now have *Stenonema ithaca* and *Stenacron canadense*. Should we continue to call them both Cahills, even though they are now of separate genera? From a practical standpoint, while such changes are of importance to entomologists, they are of little consequence to the average angler. After all, the insects themselves haven't changed, and it isn't likely the trout know of the reclassification. When in doubt, the angler's best bet is to capture one of the insects, examine it closely, and try to match it with a pattern in his box. If it works it doesn't matter whether the natural is *Stenonema* or *Stenacron*.

The species with which the Cahills are associated are extremely variable in coloration. Both entomologists Leonard and Burks, in separate books, have noted that *S. canadense* may range from nearly black in Ontario to yellow in the southern states. In Pennsylvania the Cahills are mainly pale cream in hue, with faintly mottled wings, barred legs, and two banded tails. The duns are often

Completed Palmer Cahill Dun

slow to emerge and although the hatches never seem as dense as certain others, the trout respond to their presence with enthusiasm.

The Palmer Cahill Dun is an interpretation of the pale species and has served me well for several years. The wings are cut from speckled wood duck breast feathers, although teal or other barred feathers should work equally well. Natural kapok is an ideal body material because it doesn't readily absorb water and it is easily applied to waxed thread like fur dubbing. The hackles are one each, dark cream and brown grizzly, wound from front to rear in open palmer fashion and trimmed beneath the body. This style of hackling eliminates the need of tail support and permits the use of two wood duck fibres for tails approximating those of the insect.

The Cahill hatches occur mainly in late May and early June but stragglers are often seen well into late summer, particularly as darkness approaches. It's always a pleasure to see the big, light-colored flies appear when daylight begins to fade because they generally assure a spurt of fast dry fly fishing with a visible fly to cap the day.

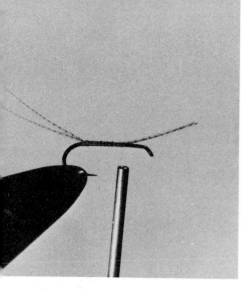

TYING A PALMER CAHILL DUN

1. Clamp a size #14 dry fly hook in vise and tie in fine, yellow tying thread at bend. For tails, tie in two barred wood duck fibres.

2. Wind thread forward about 2/3 length of shank and half-hitch. Cut a pair of matched wings from wood duck breast feathers. Finished wings should be as long as the overall hook length. Hold wings together and upright, back to back, with stems straddling shank. About 1/16 inch of bare stems should show above shank to allow for thorax dubbing. Make several figure-eight turns around stems to secure, then check alignment from front. When you are satisfied wings are perfectly straight, bend stems back under hook and wind over with several turns. Then trim off excess stems and apply a drop of hard-drying cement to bare stems at base of wings.

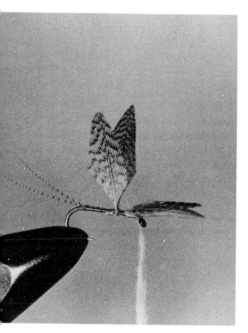

3. Select one each, dark cream and brown grizzly hackles with barbules about 1½ to 2 times as long as gap of hook. Strip off webby lower barbules and tie in hackles together, in front of wings, with figure-eight turns. Hackles should be positioned at right angles to shank, on edge and with dull sides facing eye. Bend stems along shank and bind; then trim waste stems. Wind thread forward to eye and apply a dubbing of natural kapok about 2 inches long.

4. Wind dubbed thread back to bend, forming a tapered body with thickest point at wings.

5. Grip tip of rear hackle with hackle pliers and make a complete turn in front of wings. Then wind hackle back to bend in widely spaced turns and tie off at bend. Repeat this step with the front hackle, following the path of the first. Trim excess hackle tips. Then whip-finish thread around bend behind base of tails. Apply head lacquer to finish windings.

6. Trim a wide "V" from underside of hackles.

The *Paraleptophlebia adoptiva* Dun

Gradual changes in attitude over the years are apt to go unnoticed until one glances backward. I wouldn't want to consider myself an old-timer but the years do have a way of spinning by, and I can distinctly recall, early in my fly fishing days, when a size #16 fly was considered small. Indeed, anything smaller was regarded as *frivolous*. The few fly fishermen of my acquaintance paid scant attention to the hatches of small insects; after all, no trout of respectable size could afford to expend the energy required of the rise to the surface for such small reward. And even if it did, and was so foolish as to accept a tiny artificial, the toy-like hook probably wouldn't hold. It all sounded quite reasonable until I had the privilege of watching a skilled angler destroy every shred of the anti-small hook argument.

On a balmy day in early May, the big limestone stream was seething with life. A steady procession of little slate-winged duns floated down each current tongue. Trout appeared to be rising everywhere. It was a totally new experience for me, and I was unable to cope with it. Nothing in my flybox matched the little mayflies in size and my efforts with #12s and #14s stirred nary a fin. An angler upstream was faring better and, keeping a discreet distance, we moved closer to watch. He was playing a heavy fish, which finally he netted after what seemed an interminable struggle. He kindly offered a close view of both the fish and the fly, which we accepted. In the net was the largest brown trout I had ever seen and in its jaw was firmly lodged a diminutive fly, a Blue Dun. When the angler told me it was dressed on a size #18 hook I regarded the entire performance as nothing short of miraculous. Sensing I was a neophyte, he explained that the trout were extremely selective during this hatch, a fact I had just learned, and that matching the size was just as important as duplicating color and form. It was a significant lesson, learned from an obvious master of the craft.

Quite a few years have elapsed since that revealing day in Centre County, years which have seen the development of fishing the *minutae* gradually blossom. Today a size #18 fly seems quite respectable in dimension when compared with the #22s, #24s and #28s now in rather common use. Nowhere has the refinement of this specialized form of angling been honed to a keener edge than in Pennsylvania, by brilliant anglers of the Keystone State. The principles are applicable anywhere there are rich waters and selective trout.

Looking back to the day just described, I'm reasonably certain that the little mayfly causing all the activity was *Paraleptophlebia adoptiva*, a small, brownish-bodied dun whose appearance in late April and May is heralded by many anglers in the East and Midwest. Preston Jennings regarded the species as one of questionable value, a view that many Pennsylvania fly fishermen would loudly protest. It is likely that in the streams of the Catskills where Jennings regularly fished, early season conditions of high, cold water during the emergence of *P. adoptiva* are not conducive to good dry fly fishing, regardless of the hatch of the moment.

Our pattern representing the *P. adoptiva* dun is of a design outwardly resembling the Sulphur Dun previously described. However, since it is our aim to expose the beginning fly tyer to as many techniques as possible, we have varied the tying procedure. Instead of the front-to-rear hackling as before, the two hackles are bound behind the wings at the middle of the shank, with glossy surfaces facing each other. Then the rear hackle is wound over the abdomen to the rear, tied off, and the thread is brought forward through the wound hackle, to the front hackle. The thorax is then formed and the front hackle wound forward to the head. This places the whip finish at the eye and on small hooks is a bit easier done than tying off under the tails. The result is identical in both styles of open-palmer hackling: the barbules flare forward in front and rearward in back, preserving the all-important balance of the fly on the water without the need of tail support.

Completed *Paraleptophlebia adoptiva* Dun

TYING THE *PARALEPTOPHLEBIA*
ADOPTIVA DUN

1. Clamp a size #18 dry fly hook in vise and bind fine, brown tying thread at bend. For tails tie in three medium dun hackle barbules and take a turn of thread under base of tails to flare barbules. Wind thread forward 2/3 the length of the shank and half-hitch. For wings cut a right and left quill section from a pair of matched, slate-gray mallard primaries. Trim tips round (as shown) if desired and carefully tie in wings wet fly style but with convex sides facing. Trim excess butts. Wing length should be about equal to overall length of hook.

2. (Top view) Pull wings upright and make several turns of thread behind base to secure. When satisfied that wings are straight and cocked at desired angle, with bodkin tip apply a drop of thin vinyl cement between wings at base. Then spread vinyl evenly over inside wing surfaces.

3. Select two medium dun hackles with barbule length about twice the gap of hook. Remove web near base and at middle of shank tie in front hackle on edge by its root, with glossy side facing tails. Spaced by two turns of thread, tie in rear hackle with glossy side facing eye.

4. Apply a thin dubbing of brown fur (a mixture of three parts rusty brown and one part olive) to thread and wind back to base of tails, forming a tapered abdomen. Half-hitch.

5. Wind rear hackle in open palmer fashion back to rear of abdomen and tie off over tail butts. Trim waste hackle tip.

6. Wind thread forward in spaced turns through hackle, taking care to avoid depressing barbules, to fore end of fur abdomen. Half-hitch.

7. Apply more dubbing to thread and wind forward, around base of wings, and half-hitch thread behind eye.

8. Wind front hackle forward in spaced turns. Tie off behind eye, as shown, and trim off waste tip. Whip-finish thread at head and apply head lacquer. Finally, trim a wide "V" from underside of hackle.

35

A Hendrickson Spinner

On most trout streams east of the Rockies the Hendrickson hatch is of major importance, ranking closely behind the Green Drake in the East and the "Michigan Caddis" in the Midwest. Much of the allure of the Hendrickson, at least in the northern extremities of its range, may be attributed to the fact that it is often the first hatch of the season to bring trout consistently to the surface. It appears at a time when water levels are usually beginning to recede toward normal and when stream temperatures approach the optimum for surface feeding. It is a time when trout shake off their winter lethargy and rediscover their appetites. All in all, it is an occasion to gladden the heart of the dry fly angler, whose winter-borne frustrations disappear like the melting snow banks at first sight of rising trout.

Caldwell Creek in early May

In the past, the mayfly known as the Hendrickson was identified with three separate, but closely related, species: *Ephemerella subvaria*, *E. invaria* and *E. rotunda*. All were included by Dr. Needham in the *invaria* group, which embraced eleven *Ephemerella* species. But unlike the duns, the spinners of these species are similar in general appearance, and few fly tyers, if any, make a distinction in representation. *E. subvaria* is probably the dominant species of the three; anglers know well the appearance of the smoky-winged duns and the late afternoon flights of ruddy-bodied spinners.

Typically in many *Ephemerella* species, egg-laden females curve their abdomens downward in flight with large, yellow egg sacs in prominent view. Although the egg sac is visually a dominant characteristic of the flying insect it is of dubious value in the artificial since the ovipositing females release their eggs several feet above the water. The primary period of feeding to the Hendrickson spinners occurs in late afternoon when the dying females fall helplessly to the water following oviposition. However, it has been noted by Vincent Marinaro and others that a secondary rise of trout to the same fall of spinners may occur the following morning. This is almost wholly restricted to slow-moving streams where obstructions create eddies which trap great numbers of spent insects for long periods, releasing them gradually to the current.

Our Hendrickson Spinner pattern specifically represents the female imago of *E. subvaria*, but in a slightly smaller version it is applicable to the two companion species as well. The spent wings are fashioned from hackle barbules first wound parachute-style around the base of a monofilament loop, then bunched equally. The knot in the monofilament confines the hackle within a predetermined space and prevents it from riding up the slippery nylon. When dressed as illustrated the pattern rides flush in the surface film like the spent naturals and is virtually indestructible. Durability is a necessary requisite of any spinner pattern because during the limited time of furious feeding activity—and in the failing light which usually accompanies a fall of spinners—one begrudges the time required to change a macerated fly after a trout or two.

In the Cumberland Valley of Pennsylvania, and particularly on the Yellow Breeches, the Hendrickson hatch may already be in full sway when the regular trout season opens in mid-April. Anglers in more northern climes must bide their time for awhile longer until the dogwood is in bloom and the warm glow of spring begins to assert itself. Then the dry fly fisher will know that nature has set the scene for a new angling year.

Completed Hendrickson Spinner

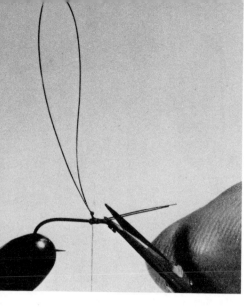

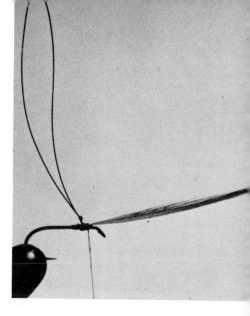

TYING A
HENDRICKSON SPINNER

1. Clamp a size #14, regular shank, dry fly hook in vise and tie in fine, brownish-olive thread well behind eye. Make a nylon loop by doubling a 6-inch strand of 5X or 6X monofilament and tying an overhand knot near the tips. Bind atop shank 1/16 inch below knot, with tips projecting over eye. Pull loop upright and wind behind. Trim excess ends of monofil, as shown.

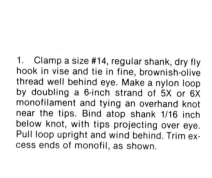

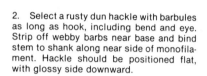

2. Select a rusty dun hackle with barbules as long as hook, including bend and eye. Strip off webby barbs near base and bind stem to shank along near side of monofilament. Hackle should be positioned flat, with glossy side downward.

3. Grasp tip of hackle in hackle pliers and wind counterclockwise around monofil beneath knot. Try to make each turn under the previous turn. Tie off in front and trim off waste hackle tip.

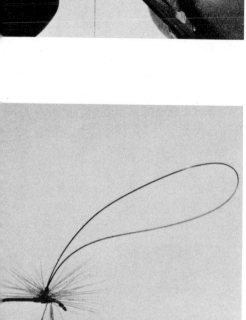

4. Separate barbules in front. Then pull loop forward and down, straddling shank behind eye. Hold loop taut in this position and tie off in front of hackle. Cut away excess monofil.

5. With moistened finger tips separate the hackle into two equal halves. Stroke barbules toward tips and roll between fingers until they approximate wing position shown. Spiral thread back to bend. Select three stiff barbules from a dun spade hackle and tie in as tails. Make a turn of thread beneath the base of tails to separate them and apply a small drop of lacquer at apex.

6. Wax a few inches of the thread next to the hook and apply a dubbing of ruddy brownish-tan fur. Wind dubbing forward to form tapered abdomen. Make a turn each snugly in back of and in front of wings, then make a figure-eight turn around base of wings. Complete thorax in front of wings and whip finish. After removing waste thread, apply lacquer to finish windings and to top of thorax over base of wings.

A *Tricorythodes* Spinner

If I were to choose a mayfly hatch that would leave the biggest void in my angling experience, should it, perish the thought, suddenly disappear from the scene, it would be the magnificent little mayflies of the genus *Tricorythodes*.

This genus was formerly included in the family Caenidae, along with the genera *Caenis* and *Brachycercus*. Characteristics shared are small size, three tails, broad wings with a dark line along the leading edge, and the absence of hind wings. The male spinners of *Tricorythodes* are primarily black or dark brown, while those of the other two genera are pale. Both *Tricorythodes* and *Brachycercus* emerge in early morning while *Caenis* generally appears in late evening and often after dark. The most definitive key is that the male *Tricorythodes* has claspers with three segments, as opposed to one. These differences may be seen in the field with the aid of a 10-power glass or at home with a wide-field microscope. In recent years, through the work of Dr. Edmunds and others, it has been determined that, despite the obvious similarities of *Tricorythodes* and *Caenis*, certain characteristics of the two indicate that their relationship is more distant than previously thought. *Tricorythodes* has therefore been removed from the family Caenidae and placed in the family Tricorythidae.

Because of the diminutive size of these insects, even when they are present in their usual vast numbers the hatches lack the dramatic visual impact of a heavy hatch of large flies. The knowledgeable fisherman watches toward the morning sun for the swarms of spinners high above the stream in anticipation of the appearance of little black and white specks on the water, which will be the spent females floating flush in the surface film. Then he knows the fun will soon begin.

The *Tricorythodes* pattern shown in the illustrations represents the female spinner with its black thorax, pale abdomen, and outspread wings. It has given me many hours of superb dry fly fishing wherever I have encountered the hatch. The pattern is easily tied but mention should be made of the somewhat unorthodox method of fashioning the wings. Two bunches of long hackle barbules are placed together, the butts of one bunch alongside the tips of the other, to form a single bundle of uniform density from end to end. Then the bundle is bound at its middle to the hook shank, in the spent position, with figure eight turns of thread. Next, both ends of the barbules are trimmed, leaving a spent wing of appropriate size extending out each side. The thread is then brought up through the wing fibres on the tyer's side, over the shank and down through the fibres on the far side. This helps to spread the barbs. Then a circular, lateral turn of thread is made under the base of the far wing, over the shank in front of the wings, under the base of the near wing and over the shank in back of the wings. The last maneuver flattens the wings and is repeated with fur-dubbed thread when the thorax is formed.

On small meadow streams the male *Tricorythodes* spinners generally fall to the grass away from the water. On the Au Sable River in Michigan, and I believe on many large streams, there is a short lull after the spent females have passed, following which many males drop to the water. This generally prompts a second rise of trout, somewhat briefer than the first, which requires a pattern with an all-black body. A corresponding male spinner pattern follows the dressing procedure of the female, substituting black tying thread, long tails of dark muskrat guard hairs, and an all-black fur body.

Tricorythodes atratus, the male spinner

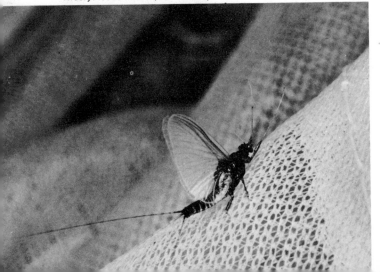

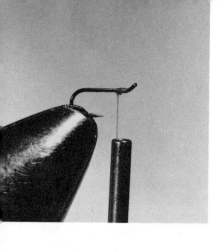

TYING A FEMALE
TRICORYTHODES SPINNER

1. Bind fine white tying thread behind the eye of a size #22 dry fly hook and half-hitch.

2. Select a large, pale dun hackle and stroke downward below the tip to cause the barbules to stand out at right angles. Remove the webby barbules from the lower hackle. Then, as shown, grasp the tips of the outstanding barbs and cut the butts near the center rib. Lay this bunch aside on a flat surface with tips protruding. Then grasp tips of barbs on remaining side of hackle and cut as before. Turn second bunch around and lay alongside first bunch, with butt ends of second even with tips of first. Then gather both bunches together as a single bundle.

3. (Top view) Lay bundle of barbules across hook at right angle in spent wing position and bind at its middle with figure-eight turns. Half-hitch. Trim ends of barbules to desired wing length, equivalent to length of hook. Then, as shown, bring thread up through barbs of near wing, over shank, and down through barbs of far wing.

4. To spread and flatten barbules, make a circular, lateral turn of thread snug under the base of the wings. (See text.)

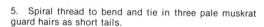

5. Spiral thread to bend and tie in three pale muskrat guard hairs as short tails.

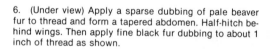

6. (Under view) Apply a sparse dubbing of pale beaver fur to thread and form a tapered abdomen. Half-hitch behind wings. Then apply fine black fur dubbing to about 1 inch of thread as shown.

7. To form thorax, wind black-dubbed thread around base of wings in figure-eight turns, then make circular, lateral turn as in step 4. Finish thorax with a turn or two in front of wings. Whip finish and cut thread. Apply a drop of black lacquer to head and a drop of thin clear lacquer to top of thorax.

8. Completed *Tricorythodes* Spinners: female on left, male on right.

An Upwing *Tricorythodes*

Although the typical posture of the mayfly spinner on the water, following ovipositing, is spent—with wings outstretched—this attitude occurs only after the dying insect loses the ability to hold its wings aloft. Particularly among small Ephemeropterans, and often in cool weather, many females spinners fall to the water and ride with erect wings for long distances, intermixed on the surface with prone spinners which fell further upstream. In such a mix I have never seen trout selective of one or the other forms, but the presence of two distinct bearings of the same spinner justifies an upwing spinner pattern to be used alternately with the spent.

I have long felt it is desirable to have alternate patterns to cope with the difficult hatches of tiny insects. This philosophy is particularly applicable to *Tricorythodes*, the little early morning mayfly. During a massive fall of *Tricorythodes* spinners, trout hang just beneath the surface, taking the tiny insects in soft rhythmic rises, as if they know the flies are helpless to leave the water. Because of the casual nature of the rise it is inevitable that a good fish is occasionally raised and scratched, the little hook failing to find a secure hold. If the trout has been feeding steadily, there is a good chance that this kind of annoyance will not put him down for long, if at all, but you may be certain that when he resumes feeding he'll be choosier than ever. Then I like to switch from the spent to the upwing pattern, or vice versa, to give our trout a fresh viewpoint to assess. If he's rested sufficiently before he begins feeding steadily again, the trout will sometimes take the new pattern on the first cast. On the other hand, if he's a crafty old veteran of previous encounters he'll take some convincing; as they say, Once hooked, twice shy. Even when my best efforts fail it's a satisfying challenge, and that, after all, is the essence of fly fishing.

Our Upwing *Tricorythodes* pattern follows the color of the female imago after she has released her eggs: black thorax and head; pale gray abdomen, wings and legs. I have had good fishing with this pattern during the emergence of *Tricorythodes* duns, too, although the fall of spinners brings on a generally more spectacular rise of trout. The pattern's dressing is relatively simple, but it is essential that the dubbing and hackling be kept sparse; otherwise, the illusion of delicacy will be lost. Starling flight feathers offer a fine-textured material for the quill wings. Sections from mallard wing feathers may be substituted, provided they are taken from the thin, lower edges of the feathers.

Windy days are always difficult times for the tiny insects. Gusts prevent the male *Tricorythodes* spinners from forming their familiar mating swarms, although at each lull they seem to appear from nowhere, only to be scattered helter-skelter by the next blow. Many are swept onto the water, and among them are female spinners with green abdomens, so colored because of the emerald egg masses not yet expelled. For these occasions I like to have on hand a variation from the regular pattern, with the abdomen dubbed of pale, olive green fur, or kapok, in lieu of gray beaver fur.

Visually following the course of a tiny flush-floating fly on the surface is never an easy matter, particularly when one's eyesight is past its prime, although *Tricorythodes* spinners are easier to see than certain others because of their contrasting light and dark coloration. On dark days, or peering upstream against a low, glaring, early morning sun, or when the trout are rising in the shadowy recesses under the cussed willow, I find I can spot the little Upwing *Tricorythodes*, with its wings silhouetted against the silvery background, more readily than low-floating types.

Female *Tricorythodes* spinner

Completed Upwing *Tricorythodes*

TYING AN UPWING
TRICORYTHODES

1. *Secure a size #22* dry fly hook in vise and bind fine, white tying thread to shank well behind eye. For wings, cut a quill section each from a left and right starling wing feather. (Thin mallard quill sections may be substituted.) Secure wings to shank wet fly style but with shiny sides together, inside.

2. Pull wings upright, make several turns of thread behind, make a loop around base and half-hitch. Separate wings with bodkin to achieve shallow angle. Apply a thin coating of vinyl cement to inside wing surfaces. Stroke leading edges of wings with black marking pen.

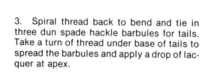

3. Spiral thread back to bend and tie in three dun spade hackle barbules for tails. Take a turn of thread under base of tails to spread the barbules and apply a drop of lacquer at apex.

4. Wax a short length of tying thread next to the shank and apply a thin dubbing of gray, natural beaver fur (or optional greenish-olive dubbing). Wind dubbing forward to form abdomen and half-hitch thread in front of wing. Now bind black tying thread to shank in front of wing, tying down white thread. Cut and remove unused white thread as shown.

5. Select a medium or pale dun hackle with barbs 1½ to 2 times as long as hook gap. Remove webby lower barbs and tie in vertically behind wings so that hackle extends downward under hook with glossy side toward eye. Apply a small amount of fine black dubbing fur or kapok to thread and wind forward to form thorax.

6. Wind hackle, making one turn behind and one turn in front of wings; tie off and cut excess hackle tip. Whip finish, remove thread, and apply head lacquer to finish windings. After clipping out a "V" in underside of hackle, the Upwing *Thicorythodes* is completed.

An *Isonychia* Spinner

In the vernacular of the fly fisher the big mayflies of the genus *Isonychia* are variously referred to as Leadwing Coachmen, Leadwing Drakes, White-Gloved Howdies, Maroon Drakes and Mahogany Drakes. The spinners are beautiful insects and, unlike many duns of this genus, are fast, graceful fliers. Mating flights generally occur in the evening and the females return to the stream just before dusk to lay their eggs in aerated riffles. As some of the common names would seem to imply, many of these flies have bodies of rich, reddish-brown coloration—an almost incandescent blush that is further accentuated by the warm, low-angled light rays of evening. The spinner fall is often of short duration but the surface feeding it induces is worthy of the angler's attention. The flies come on the water at a time when the bigger fish are shaking off their daytime lethargy in anticipation of their evening meal.

Detached bodies—or extended bodies, as they are sometimes called—have been in use for a long time. Fly dressers have concocted several methods to achieve this effect. In the early days of the dry fly an appropriate length of silkworm gut was bound to the hook, extending rearward over the bend. Tails were affixed to the end of the short gut strand and a fur dubbing was applied, forming a tapered abdomen, over which a ribbing material was often wound to represent the segmentation. With the substitution of nylon monofilament for gut, this method is still in use today. Schwiebert describes the dressing of fur bodies on a strand of aluminum wire stretched between two vises. Detached bodies of bound deer hair are common in the Midwest, particularly to represent the big *Hexagenia* mayflies. An interesting departure is the English Flybody hook, in which the base for the detached body is an extension of the hook itself.

Theoretically, the detached body shows its best advantage in large flies. It permits a body of correct size to be dressed on a short-shanked hook of one nominal size smaller than if the body were dressed conventionally on a regular-shanked hook. Thus, a fly with the dimensions of, say, a conventional size #10 may be dressed with a detached body on a size #12, 4X short hook, reducing overall weight and enhancing the fly's floatability.

Our *Isonychia* Spinner pattern uses still another type of detached body, fashioned from a large hackle tip with a section of barbules inverted, coated lightly with adhesive and rolled. The tacky barbules adhere to each other, creating a tapered bundle which may be pressed between fingertips to a flattish form of the desired width. The tip of the feather is then cut and removed, leaving two uninverted barbules to serve as tails. Vinyl cement is recommended for the adhesive coating because it remains flexible when dry. Pliobond (Wilhold) is excellent for this purpose, too, and its tan hue does not affect the red-brown color of the detached body.

The spent wings are formed by winding a large dun hackle parachute-style around a doubled monofilament post and bunching the barbules. The thorax is fashioned of reddish-brown dubbing, wound around and over the base of the wings.

One evening last season I was on the big stream when the *Isonychia* spinners began to appear in the air. I bent on the spent pattern and stationed myself near the head of a large pool, within reach of the riffle above, where I hoped the females would soon begin their egg laying. A movement to my right caught my eye and in the fading light I could barely distinguish the form of a foot-long trout, lying in feeding position in a shallow run next to the bank. I cast the fly well above the trout but it never reached him for it was intercepted in the turbulent water above by a trout of heftier proportions. The hooked fish was wild and nearly unmanageable, giving the impression that it was either a giant or a lesser fish hooked in the tail. He made a looping run above me and was halfway into the pool below when I decided I'd better give chase. Splashing and slithering over mossy rocks in the shallow water, I miraculously kept my footing and we had it out downstream. When I finally netted him I found he was neither the leviathan I had anticipated, nor was he foul-hooked. He was a well-proportioned, highly spirited brown trout of 16½ inches, with the *Isonychia* Spinner hooked firmly in the corner of his jaw. Not quite as big as I had expected, perhaps, but a fun fish with which to end a pleasant day.

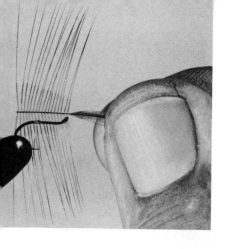

TYING AN *ISONYCHIA* SPINNER

1.   Clamp a size #12, 4X short hook in vise. For detached body, select a rather large, reddish-brown hackle and cut the stem about 2 inches below the tip. Hold hackle alongside hook for scale and stroke barbules to stand at right angles for a length along the stem equivalent to the overall length of hook.

2.   Stroke the separated barbules downward until they are parallel with stem. Hold by tips of barbules in this position. Then apply a thin coat of vinyl cement or Pliobond to the dull side of inverted barbules, as shown.

3.   When adhesive becomes tacky, roll coated barbules along stem to form a tapered cylinder. Then flatten between fingertips. For tails, separate the two outer uninverted barbules and cut off remainder of hackle tip.

4.   Tie in brown thread and bind detached body to hook in position shown. For maximum flexibility, bind barbules only, at a point just beyond cut end of stem. Trim excess barbules and wind thread forward a few turns. Then double a 5-inch strand of 4X monofilament and tie an overhand knot near the tips, forming a loop. Bind monofil ends to top of shank and pull loop upright, with knot about 1/16 inch above shank. Trim excess tips of monofil.

5.   Select a medium dun hackle (preferably a spade) with barbule length equivalent to length of fly, from eye to base of tails. Strip off lower webby portion of hackle and bind stem to hook against base of monofil. Hackle should be positioned flat, with glossy side down. Attach hackle pliers to tip and wind, parachute-style, counterclockwise around monofil below knot, winding each turn underneath preceding turn. Tie off in front and trim excess.

6.   Pull monifil loop smartly forward, over eye and down, straddling shank and separating hackle in front. Hold loop taut in this position and tie off monofil. Trim excess.

7.   Separate the wound hackle into two equal halves and stroke each half toward tips until rough simulation of spent wings is achieved. Then bring thread back to base of detached body and apply dubbing of reddish-brown fur or synthetic. Wind dubbing forward to press against rear of wings; then take a turn against front of wings and make figure-eight turns around wing base. Finally, wind dubbing to eye and whip finish thread. Apply a drop of lacquer to top of thorax and to head.

8.   Completed *Isonychia* Spinner.

43

The Blue-Winged Olive Dun

Even the most traditional fly patterns can be the source of a new idea or an improvement. For the Pennsylvania Hendrickson hatches I often fish a dry-fly pattern which, for want of a better name, I called an Olive Hendrickson. The fly, which bears no resemblance to the Hendrickson pattern of the Catskills, has a body of ruddy brownish-olive rabbit fur, shaped wings of dark mallard primary sections and mixed olive and rusty dun hackles, sparsely palmered and clipped on the bottom. Why an *Olive* Hendrickson?

For some strange reason the use of olive-tinted hackles in the traditional American dry fly patterns is rare. It is difficult to understand because many of our mayflies of medium to large size carry a distinct olive hue in body and/or leg coloration. This category of insects is quite apart from, and in addition to, the Little Olives of the genus *Baetis*. Michigan entomologist Dr. Justin Leonard has designated the subimagos of the entire genus *Ephemerella* as Blue-Winged Olive Duns, borrowing the English denomination of *E. ignita*, the famous B.W.O. of angling literature. In the eastern United States, *Ephemerella attenuata* is fairly common and fits this designation perfectly, as does the smaller *E. lata* of the Midwest. On Michigan's Au Sable River I have fished many times over trout feeding selectively to the latter and have at least convinced myself that hackles with an olive cast are infinitely superior, if not essential during this hatch.

Of the several species loosely referred to as Hendricksons, *Ephemerella subvaria* is predominant. Like most mayflies, the Hendricksons are apt to show subtle color variations from stream to stream, or indeed on different sections of the same stream, and often they exhibit an olive overtone in body and legs, especially when viewed closely in transmitted light. Other genera come to mind, too, like *Leptophlebia* and *Paraleptophlebia*, which have species fitting the description of Blue-Winged Olives.

The Blue-Winged Olive pattern illustrated specifically represents *E. attenuata*; however, with modifications in size and coloration it serves to represent any of the Blue-Winged Olive duns. The hackle combination in all is a mixture of medium olive with medium rusty dun, producing a soft greenish-gray effect, with a subtle brownish wash. Bright green hackles should be avoided but even these may be toned and made usable by stroking the barbules with a brown or dark yellow colorfast marking pen with felt tip. This is an emergency measure requiring a little experimentation with a waste hackle before applying it to a finished fly.

Completed Blue-Winged Olive Dun

Ephemerella attenuata

With the effective waterproofing available for dry flies nowadays, almost any fur, or even wool, may be used for body dubbing. White rabbit fur may be dyed easily with household dyes and various shades are achieved by blending plucked fur of different colors with the dubbing needle. Even more convenient is the use of pre-dyed angora yarn or the spun furs available from fly tying material suppliers. The latter are plucked from the skein and mixed to the desired shade. A mixture of three parts olive and one part brown dubbing will satisfy the body requirements of most of the Blue-Winged Olives. However, for the Hendrickson I prefer three parts reddish-brown and one part olive.

The pattern is flexible and easily modified but as always, close examination of the naturals on your stream provides the soundest basis for dressing the artificial. Sizes range from #14 for the largest Hendricksons to #20 for the smaller species of *Paraleptophlebia*.

TYING A BLUE-WINGED OLIVE DUN

1. Bind fine tying thread (Danville prewaxed olive shown) at the bend of a size #16 dry fly hook and tie in three wood duck fibres as tails. Wind thread forward and half-hitch at position shown.

2. For wings cut matched quill sections from a right and left duck primary and tie in, wet fly style. Trim tips to shape if desired.

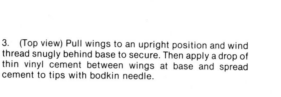

3. (Top view) Pull wings to an upright position and wind thread snugly behind base to secure. Then apply a drop of thin vinyl cement between wings at base and spread cement to tips with bodkin needle.

4. Select one each medium olive and medium rusty dun hackles with barbule length of 1½ to 2 times the gap of hook. Bind to shank perpendicularly in front of wings, with glossy sides facing rear and edges facing tyer. Bind roots forward under shank and trim off waste.

5. Wax a portion of thread next to the hook and apply a brownish olive dubbing. (See text.) Wind dubbing toward bend, tapering abdomen at rear, and half-hitch thread just forward of tail base.

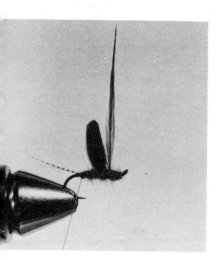 

6. Winding hackles individually, make a full turn in front of wings, then wind in spaced turns over abdomen to rear. Tie off each hackle at end of body and trim waste tips.

7. Whip finish (or half-hitch several times) around bend underneath base of tails. Press finish windings against tail base, causing tail fibres to separate and flare upwards. Trim off waste thread.

8. (Bottom view) With fine-pointed scissors, trim hackle close to underside of body, leaving a broad, inverted "V" from front to rear. Finally, apply lacquer to finish windings.

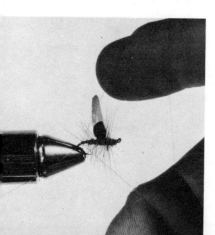 

45

The *Baetis* Spinners

Trout seem to be particularly fond of the little, two-tailed mayflies of the genus *Baetis*. The duns generally appear sporadically during daylight hours. Despite their small size, they are fairly easy to see on the water because their upright, smoky-gray wings flash in the sunlight. The fall of *Baetis* spinners is another matter, particularly when it comes in the waning hours of daylight. Like any small, flush-floating insects, *Baetis* spinners are difficult to detect on the water in failing light. Often the trout offer the first clue that a spinner fall is developing when they begin rising in quiet, rhythmic fashion.

Fishing the tiny spent spinners at dusk is almost like fishing after dark; the precise placement of the fly depends more on instinct than on sight for it is rare that the low-floating fly can be seen at this hour. If the stream is not in shadow the angler can sometimes see the silhouette of his leader on the silvery surface, and this is an aid in locating one's fly. Even without the visual advantage it is surprising how effectively one adapts to fishing at twilight, casting from judgment alone. Random casting is rarely beneficial; one's attention should be concentrated on a specific rising trout. Each rise should be treated as if it were to the fly, and if indeed it is, only a gentle lift of the rod tip is necessary to make connection.

A couple of years ago we encountered a rather heavy fall of *Baetis levitans* spinners on Falling Springs. We were fishing a narrow stretch, and the trout were lined up along the grassy banks, sipping the drifting insects with metronomic precision. Casts were timed so that the fly would pass over the trout at the moment it was ready to take another spinner, hoping he would take mine

Completed *Baetis* Spinner

instead. It was entirely guesswork in the dim light because I couldn't see my fly, but evidently I was doing something right for on every third or fourth lift I found myself attached to a solidly hooked trout.

Although the color of male *Baetis* spinners varies among the various species, the females generally have brown to brownish-olive bodies. This is a fortunate circumstance because it lessens the number of patterns required to cover several species. The *Baetis* Spinner pattern matches the female imagos of many species of this genus, provided it is dressed in sizes #20 and #22. The spent wings are fashioned from two small bunches of medium dun hackle barbules laid together to form a single bunch. The tips of one bunch are matched to the butts of the other and the barbs are mixed. This gives both wings a uniform density which would be lacking if one wing had only barbule tips and the other, butts.

The hair tamper illustrated in the tying sequence was made by cementing four short sections of plastic tubing vertically in the corners of a shallow lid from a small plastic box. In mine the tubes are 3/16 inch to 1/2 inch in diameter and 3/8 to 1 inch in height; however, these may be varied according to one's individual requirements. It's a handy little gadget, not only for matching the tips of hackle barbs but for hair wings as well. Simply insert hair or barbules into the tube of appropriate size and tap the tamper on a hard surface. When withdrawn, the tips of the wing material should be perfectly matched.

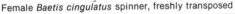
Female *Baetis cingulatus* spinner, freshly transposed

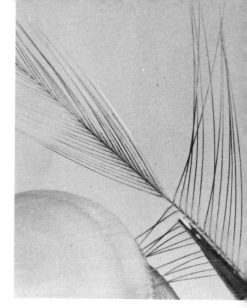

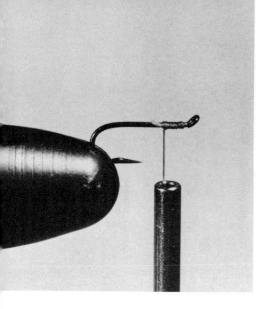

TYING THE *BAETIS* SPINNER

1. Bind fine, olive tying thread well behind the eye of a light-wire hook. Sizes #20 and #22 are useful.

2. Then, select a fairly large medium dun hackle and stroke downward below tip, causing barbs to stand out at right angles. Separate about twelve to fifteen barbs and grasp them by the tips. Cut the butts near the center rib and place the bunch, tips down, in the smallest tube of the hair tamper. Then turn the hackle around and cut an equal number of barbs from the opposite side of the rib.

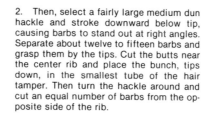

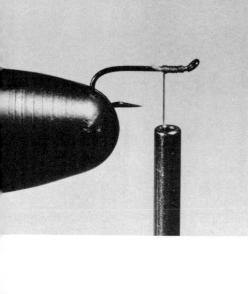

3. Place this bunch in the tamper with butts down. Mix the barbules in the tamper, tap it on a hard surface to make ends even, and remove bunch. Lacking a tamper, match tips of one bunch with butts of other and mix by hand.

4. Bind combined barbules to top of hook at center of bunch with figure-eight turns. Trim ends of barbs to finished wing length, equal to length of hook. Then bring thread up through barbs on near side, over shank and down through barbs on far side. Then make a lateral turn snug under base of wings, flattening wings and spreading barbules.

5. Wind thread to bend and tie in two dun barbules for tails. Then wax about 3 inches of the thread next to the hook and apply a dubbing of brown fur on synthetic. Wind dubbing forward to form tapered abdomen.

6. Make a lateral turn of dubbed thread under base of wings, then make a figure-eight turn around wings. Complete thorax in front of wings. After whip finishing head, remove thread and apply a drop of lacquer to finish winds and to top of thorax.

The Green Drake Dun

In the British Isles three closely related species of Ephemera are known as the Green Drake, of which *E. danica* is most predominant. American anglers borrowed the common name from their British cousins and applied it to *Ephemerella guttulata*, principally because of its size and superficial resemblance to its British counterpart. The big Green Drake often stimulates an orgy of feeding fish unparalleled by other mayflies, frequently inspiring large trout to throw aside their usual caution and to surface feed in broad daylight with uncommon abandon.

There is a color variation in the Green Drake dun from stream to stream but even when it is most descriptive of its appellation the beginning fly fisher, expecting a distinctly green insect, often wonders how on earth it ever got its name. Remembering that the name was borrowed from the English fly, a clue may be found in the seventeenth century writings of Charles Cotton, who observed that "his tail turns up towards his back like a mallard; from whence, questionless, he has his name of the Green-Drake."

As might be expected in a fly as large as the Green Drake (the wing height and body length may reach one inch), there are several problems attendant to the dressing of a dry fly representation believable to the trout. First, if tied to size in the conventional way the hook required would be very large for a dry fly, producing excess weight and inhibiting good flotation. Next, if you will watch the dun on the water you'll note that its abdomen and tails curve upward away from the surface. This attitude requires a dry that will balance properly without tail support. Finally, the big wings of the natural are far too prominent to be denied and the wing material must show a tall, broad outline.

The first two problems were overcome by the use of a flexible detached body and an unusual method of hackling. The bound deer or elk hair body gives the fly its required length but permits the use of a fine-wire size #12 hook with a shank a little shorter than normal. The dubbed portion of the body becomes the fly's thorax while the detached part extending from the hook is its abdomen. To give the fly balance on the water an initial half-turn of hackle is made *laterally* under the base of the detached body, after which the hackles are wound in open palmer fashion and clipped underneath. The lateral half-turn of hackle behind the hook balances the fly perfectly at its heaviest point, preventing the abdomen from tipping backwards and touching the surface.

The wings are trimmed to shape with toenail clippers from two mottled back feathers of a ring-neck pheasant. Since these feathers are curved in profile, rendering them difficult to hold flat, back to back, they must be shaped individually. Because of their broad surfaces it is essential that the wings be set in perfect alignment, which can be ascertained by sighting along the fly from front to rear. Using the eye of the hook as a sight, simply align the bend in the eye; if the wings appear as thin slivers they are straight. A drop of hard-drying cement applied to the bare stems at the base of the wings will hold them in position.

I had the experience of fishing three wet, miserable, wonderful days to the Green Drake hatch on Young Woman's Creek. It rained continuously the whole time; the stream reached three distinct levels: high, higher, and ridiculous. But the water remained clear and we fished the big detached body dries as if we didn't know better. In three days we caught and released more trout than I would have dreamed lived in that stretch of stream. The average size was such that the three of us are reluctant to mention it aloud, lest we be labeled tellers of tall tales.

Female *Ephemera guttulata* dun

Completed Green Drake Dun, showing its floating position on water

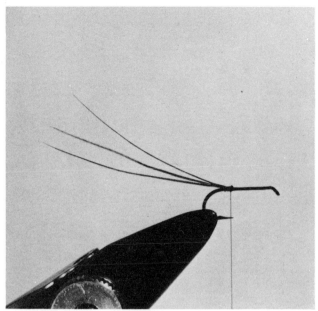

1.   Clamp on a size #12 dry fly hook in vise and tie in fine, tan thread (Herb Howard 7/0) at bend. For tails tie in three long, reddish fibres from a ring-neck pheasant's tail feather. Tails should be three to four times the length of hook shank.

2.   Cut a bunch of buff-colored deer or elk body hair from the hide (bunch should be about 3/16 inch wide when flattened) and remove fuzz and short hairs. Cut off tips of hair so that bunch is slightly shorter than tails. Hold hair in rocker grip over tie-in point, with 1/8 inch of butts projecting toward eye. Then make a firm, steady turn of thread around hair and shank, flaring hair butts. Maintaining firm tension, make a second turn; then wind forward through flared butts and back again, binding down individual butts. Half-hitch.

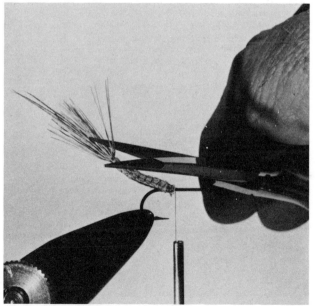

3.   Stroke hair to remove slack and arrange in a bundle with tails enclosed within. Hold hair in place with left hand and with right, make spaced turns of thread to simulate body segments. As each turn is made you will have to pass the bobbin underneath the left hand and over the vise but you may manipulate your left forefinger to hold each turn in place as you progress. Decrease the width of the segments as you approach the end of the abdomen and increase thread tension to achieve a tapered effect. After you have wrapped a distance of roughly the overall length of the hook, make an extra turn of thread over the last and reverse directions, wrapping back to the hook over previous winds in a cross pattern. Half-hitch just forward of hair tie-in.

4.   With fine-pointed scissors carefully trim away ends of hair, leaving only tails extending from rear of body.

5. For wings select two mottled feathers from a pheasant's back and individually trim to shape with toenail clippers. Effective wing height should be equivalent to overall body length, from eye to end of abdomen. Hold wings in position, back to back with stems straddling shank, and bind stems to shank with figure-eight turns. A bit of bare stems should show above shank to permit thorax dubbing. Bend ends of stems back along underside of shank and bind in this position. Trim off excess stems. Adjust wings by preening until they are perfectly straight. Then apply a drop of hard-drying cement to stems at base of wings.

6. Select a stiff brown-barred grizzly hackle (Rhode Island Red may be substituted) with barbules slightly longer than gap of hook. Tie in hackle on edge just behind wings with glossy side facing bend. Then spiral thread to rear and tie in one cream and one grizzly hackle similar in size to front hackle. Rear hackles should be tied in flat, with glossy sides down and grizzly hackle uppermost, both pointing away from tyer.

7. Grasp tips of rear hackles with fingers and make a lateral half-turn to the left, passing under base of detached body and ending on near side of fly. Bind down with two turns just ahead of spread barbules.

8. With tweezers carefully bend free portion of rear hackles so that they stand on edge and point toward tyer.

50

9. Wax 2 inches of the tying thread next to the hook and apply a full dubbing of yellow-dyed kapok or fur. Wind dubbing forward, ending with one turn in front of wings.

10. Individually wind the two rear hackles forward in spaced palmer fashion and tie off each in front of wings. Then take one full turn of the front hackle behind wings and one turn in front. Tie off and trim away waste hackle tips.

11. Again apply dubbing to thread and wind forward to eye. Whip finish thread behind eye and apply a drop of head lacquer to finish.

12. (Front view) With scissors trim away the underside of the palmered hackle, leaving an open, inverted "V." Be careful to avoid cutting lateral barbules in rear.

The Coffin Fly Spinner

The spinner or imago stage of the Green Drake is known variously as the Gray Drake, Black Drake, or Coffin Fly but the last appears to have gained widest acceptance, mainly because of the fly's eerie appearance in flight. With its dark wings and contrasting white body, the Coffin Fly is visible for long distances in the diminishing light of evening. So dramatic is the Green Drake's change in appearance after transposition from dun to spinner that many anglers think of the two stages as two distinct insects.

Numerically, the emergence of Green Drake duns is rarely as impressive as the fall of spinners. On streams where the hatch is considered sparse the emergence of duns may begin relatively early in the day and continue until late afternoon, with few emerging flies visible to the angler at a given time. To the casual observer it would seem unlikely that such a meager showing could be called a hatch, but the accumulation of duns over the course of the day can be appreciated by inspecting the foliage along the stream late in the afternoon. Then, when the great flights of spinners assemble in the evening, one gets a true picture of the magnitude of the hatch.

Knowing that a heavy fall of Coffin Fly spinners will bring large trout to the surface, many veteran Green Drake anglers prefer to choose a known location of a big fish and to wait until it starts feeding steadily before beginning to cast. It's sound strategy because random casting —or the commotion caused by landing lesser trout—will often keep the big one down. Too, it's a good idea to have several such places in mind in the event that the spinners don't come down at the first location. The spinner fall is not necessarily uniform over the entire stream, nor does the appearance of Coffin Flies in the air guarantee they will be on the water the same evening.

Once, on a Clinton County stream, I had chosen a fine pool for my evening fishing, a pool where I knew several good trout resided. Barely mustering enough willpower to resist fishing when the spinners appeared on schedule, I scanned the water until at last I found what I'd hoped to see: a pointed snout silently parted the surface behind a boulder and a Coffin Fly disappeared. Then it happened again and I knew it was time to end my vigil and begin fishing.

The next hour was a busy one for I had the good fortune to land four exceptional brown trout, all rising in the same quiet, unobstrusive manner at their chosen stations. At dusk I had a brief encounter with a fifth trout which promptly frayed my leader on a sunken boulder and broke away.

Unlike the Green Drake dun, the Coffin Fly spinner floats flush on the surface film, assuming the spent attitude typical of the dying female imago following egg-laying. The imprint made on the surface by the prone body and wings of the spinner is totally different from that of the dun, whose abdomen and wings are held clear of the water. The difference is recognizable by trout and a successful spinner pattern demands the flat-floating characteristics of the natural.

The Coffin Fly spinner pattern shown in the photo sequence is the product of much experimentation. The general design may be used to represent any and all mayfly spinners, provided appropriate adjustments are made to match size and color. The detached body is made by reversing the barbules of a large hackle, coating the inside surface with vinyl cement, and after the tails have been set in place, rolling the hackle between the fingertips. Rolling causes the tacky barbules to adhere to each other longitudinally around the center rib in a tapered, cylindrical form. The result is a completely flexible body of the desired shape and translucency.

The broad, flat wings are formed from hackle wound parachute style around the base of a monofilament loop and bunched. A knot in the doubled monofilament positioned about $1/16$ inch above the shank prevents the wound hackle from riding up the monofil, confining the turns close to the hook. The completed fly is a good floater, extremely light in weight and almost indestructible.

Female imago of *Stenonema vicarium*

TYING THE COFFIN
FLY SPINNER

1. Prepare a detached body as follows. Select a large white hackle and hold it with dull side toward you. Stroke barbules below the tip toward hackle butt and hold in position shown. Adjust hold so that the length of center rib between thumb and barbule separation is equal to full length of a size #12 dry fly hook, including eye and bend. With point of scissors cut center rib next to thumb, as shown, and with right hand reach under and remove severed hackle butt. For tails select three straight black bear hairs (or black hackle barbules) and lay them aside.

2. With bodkin needle coat the reversed barbules to thumb with vinyl cement and quickly set tails in cement at position shown. Hold in this position until cement begins to lose glaze.

3. Then roll hackle between thumb and forefinger, making certain that tail butts are enclosed at end. Tacky cement adheres barbules around center rib, forming tapered cylinder. Flatten body slightly for desired breadth.

4. With tweezers bend hackle tip away from tails and cut off next to formed body as shown.

5. Place size #12 hook in vise, tie in fine yellow thread in front of bend and bind detached body to hook. For maximum flexibility only the bunched barbules, not the center rib, should be bound. Trim away barbule tips.

6. Double a 5-inch strand of 4X (.007) monofilament nylon and tie a knot near the tips. Bind tips of nylon along top of hook at a point midway between eye and detached body. Pull formed loop upright and secure with turns behind base. Knot should be about 1/16 inch above shank. Select one black and one grizzly hackle (stiff) with barbs about three times length of shank. Bind to top of hook just behind base of nylon. Hackles should be positioned flat, with glossy sides down, black hackle above.

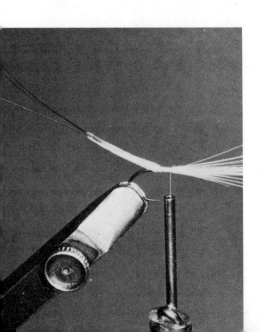

7. Grasp tips of both hackles lengthwise with hackle pliers and wind together around nylon base, below knot, in counterclockwise direction. After last turn tie off hackles in front, half-hitch and trim off waste tips.

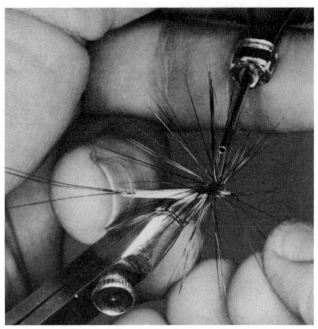

8. Separate barbules in front and pull nylon loop forward and down, with the two strands straddling the hook. Tie off in this position and trim away excess nylon.

9. Wax a few inches of thread next to the hook. To achieve a mottled thorax apply a dubbing of alternating small bunches of black and yellow kapok (or spun fur) to the thread. Make one turn of dubbed thread tight against the front of the hackle and allow the thread to hang while you separate the barbules in black. Then move dubbed thread under and behind hackle, taking a turn snug against the rear edge of hackle and another to the base of the detached body. Finally, wind forward again, make one figure-eight turn over the base of the hackle wings and end with thread behind eye. Whip finish and lacquer head.

10. Completed Coffin Fly Spinners.

The Great Red Spinner

On most trout streams there is a rather predictable progression of insect hatches from the season's beginning to its end. True, there are times when the hatches are sparse; but, on the other hand, there are several weeks when the variety of insects is so great that the angler doesn't dare leave a fly pattern at home. Particularly crowded in the northeastern emergence calendar is the period from mid-May through early June, when Sulphurs, *Perla* stoneflies, March Browns, Green Drakes, Brown Drakes, Ginger Quills, Brown Quills, and caddisflies of several species—and this is only a partial list—are on the wing.

Stenonema vicarium, the American March Brown and its imago, the Great Red Spinner, generally precede by a few days the emergence of the Green Drake and often the appearance of the two species overlaps. When this occurs, *S. vicarium* is often relegated to a secondary position because of the Green Drake's dramatic entry onto the scene. Nevertheless, without the competition of the Green Drake, *S. vicarium* is an impressive hatch capable of drawing the attention of large trout. I have been on Penn's Creek in late May when the evening air was literally filled with the mating swarms of Great Red Spinners. At first they are seen above the tree tops, hovering almost motionless, as if suspended by invisible strands; then, gradually they descend to the water and ovipositing begins. There are times when the descent stops at about ten feet above the water and suddenly the spinners disappear, evidently choosing to return at another time when conditions are more to their liking.

The Great Red Spinner is a handsome insect with barred legs typical of its genus, a tan abdomen with dark brown bands between segments, and large wings which characteristically slope backwards. Although the wings are clear, the veins are sharply outlined in fine lines of blackish brown.

Our pattern described here represents the spent Great Red Spinner. As with previous spinner patterns, the wings are fashioned by winding a hackle parachute-style around an anchor of monofilament. The barbules are then separated into two halves, stroked and rolled between the fingertips until they achieve the posture of the natural's outspread wings. Crisscross turns of thread lock the wings in position and they are further secured by similar treatment when the fur-dubbed thread is wound forward to form the thorax. If you are one of these fortunates who own (and if so, probably hoard) a cape from an ancient Barred Rock rooster you have the perfect hackle for the wings of this pattern. On the

Female imago of *Ephemera guttulata*

really old birds the black begins to take on a rusty tinge which closely matches the wing veins of the natural. If you haven't such vintage hackle, don't worry about it. Run-of-the-mill grizzly works fine, too. A single spade hackle of appropriate size furnishes the material for both wings and tails.

Since the Great Red Spinner often returns to the water at a time when other flies are emerging, identifying what a specific trout is taking can sometimes be a problem. By watching carefully the angler can generally ascertain the splashy rise to a fluttering caddis or to the drifting dun. But the clue to the spinner rise is the soft ring appearing in flat water away from the heaviest flow. It often occurs just before dark. The quiet, subtle rises sometimes belie the size of the trout, which take the prone spinners casually as if they know they are powerless to fly away.

TYING THE GREAT RED SPINNER

1. Clamp a size #12 dry fly hook in vise and bind fine, yellow tying thread to the shank well behind eye. Double a 6-inch strand of 4X monofilament and tie an overhand knot near the tips, forming a loop. Bind to shank with tips extending over eye, allowing about 1/16 inch between knot and shank. (The knot prevents the hackle from riding up the slippery monofil.) Pull loop upright and bind in vertical position, then cut off excess ends of monofil. Select a grizzly spade hackle with barbules as long as the overall hook length. Remove web and bind to hook with glossy side down in position shown.

2. Grip tip of hackle in hackle pliers and wind counterclockwise around monofilament post, positioning each turn under the previous turn. After last turn, raise barbules in front out of the way and tie off with several turns. Cut off excess hackle tip. Then separate barbules in front and pull loop firmly over eye and downward, the two strands straddling the shank. Tie off strands snugly against base of hackle and remove excess monofil.

3. Arrange barbules into two equal bunches. Alternately stroke each bunch and roll between moistened fingertips. Then make several figure-eight turns of thread around base of wings. For ribbing cut a short length of brown nymph thread and bind one end underneath shank behind wings. Then bind ribbing thread underneath shank to bend and half-hitch.

4. For tails, tie in four grizzly spade barbules. Make a turn or two underneath base of tails and divide barbules to achieve angle shown. Apply a drop of head lacquer to base of tails.

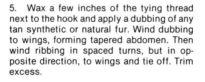

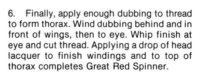

5. Wax a few inches of the tying thread next to the hook and apply a dubbing of any tan synthetic or natural fur. Wind dubbing to wings, forming tapered abdomen. Then wind ribbing in spaced turns, but in opposite direction, to wings and tie off. Trim excess.

6. Finally, apply enough dubbing to thread to form thorax. Wind dubbing behind and in front of wings, then to eye. Whip finish at eye and cut thread. Applying a drop of head lacquer to finish windings and to top of thorax completes Great Red Spinner.

Adult Stoneflies and Caddisflies

The order Plecoptera is represented by stoneflies, the immature forms of which require running water and are therefore not found in lakes. They are particularly plentiful in streams of moderately steep gradient where abundant aeration apparently suits their requirements. There are over 200 stonefly species in North America.

Adult stoneflies are four-winged insects. At rest they fold their wings flat over their bodies with the tips protruding beyond the posterior end of the abdomen. Characteristically, they have two tails, but in a few species the tails are vestigial and resemble short horns. The flight of the stonefly is steady and slow and in large species, laborious.

Caddisflies or sedges (also called rails in Ireland) belong to the order Trichoptera. Their species outnumber both mayflies and stoneflies, and while they are thought by some to resemble moths in flight, a distinction between the two is easily made when they are observed at rest.

Four-winged insects, caddisflies fold their wings in rooflike fashion over their bodies and the wings are covered with minute hairs. Although they do not have tails they carry long antennae, sometimes considerably longer than the insects themselves. Unlike mayflies and stoneflies, caddisflies experience complete metamorphosis, undergoing the stages of egg, larva, pupa, and winged adult.

Despite the recognition long given caddisflies by the British on their waters, until relatively recent years American anglers have neglected to give these insects the attention they deserve. Adult stoneflies have fared even worse, except for the massive hatches of giant *Pteronarcys*, the "salmon flies" of western streams—events that could hardly go unnoticed. Fortunately, anglers are now giving these important insects their due and appropriate patterns are finding permanent residence in their flyboxes.

The Little Black Stonefly

The little black stoneflies of the genus *Capnia*, along with those of *Taeniopteryx*, are common on many of our trout streams early in the season. Anglers who frequent the streams during late winter are likely to find them in fair numbers in the latter part of February or in March. When weather and water conditions are favorable an ensuing rise of trout is not uncommon. This is a real bonus for the cold weather fly fisher; the chance to fish dry on a bright day, if only briefly, is a nice respite from the usual streamer fly or the deeply sunken nymph.

Capnia vernalis is a common eastern species and it is somewhat smaller than the familiar species of *Taeniopteryx*. These are amiable little creatures which may often be seen crawling along one's shirt sleeve as if to give the angler a clue as to the fly of the moment. *C. vernalis* has a shiny black head and thorax, a ruddy brown abdomen, and distinctively veined blackish wings which, like all stoneflies, lie flat over the insect's back when at rest. Its legs are dark brown and the long antennae seem never to be still, constantly sweeping from side to side in a restless, searching motion.

Although the primary hatches of the little black stoneflies generally end by mid-May there seem to be many stragglers which appear sporadically in the summer months, and I have observed them as late as August. Thus, a representative pattern in appropriate size may be useful over much of the season and not limited to the early period of major activity. Our Little Black Stonefly has proved its worth as a dry fly not only when *Capnia* or *Taeniopteryx* were in evidence but on occasions when few insects were on the water.

There are several possible approaches to representing any of the Plecoptera as a dry fly and of initial importance are the posture and profile of the fly on the water. Unlike the mayfly dun, which floats with its wings erect, the stonefly assumes a squat, low-riding attitude which denies utilizing the design of the traditional dry fly. Instead, the hackling should balance the fly, both front and rear, without requiring tail support. In this instance hackles of the darkest chocolate brown are tied fore and aft, facing opposite directions, and trimmed top and bottom to leave only a spray of barbules extending out the sides. Although stoneflies have two tails they are obscured by the overhang of the folded wings and have been omitted in the pattern. Likewise, the antennae have been eliminated since they serve no function in a small dry fly.

The flat wings extending over the back of the insect may be represented by hackle tips, hair, bunched hackle barbules, or other materials but I have found nothing so satisfying as a single Wonder Wing, thinly coated with vinyl cement for durability. The rounded tip of the Wonder Wing conforms to the shape of the prototype and the spacing of the reversed barbules provides translucency and a suggestion of vein pattern. Best of all, it retains its shape and silhouette after repeated use and is far superior in this respect to hackle tips, which tend to become mere slivers after repeated wettings.

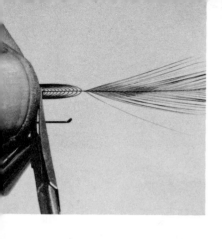

TYING THE LITTLE BLACK STONEFLY

1. Clamp a size #20 dry fly hook in vise. Then make a Wonder Wing by stroking a large, black hackle toward its root, inverting the barbules below the tip. With the hook as reference, measure wing length equal to length of hook, including eye and bend. With fine-pointed scissors sever the center rib (close to thumb as shown) without cutting barbules. Remove waste lower portion of hackle. Without relaxing left hand grip, spread vinyl cement thinly over wing with bodkin point. Hold near heat of work lamp to expedite drying.

2. When cement has begun to set, transfer wing to a spare hackle plier and set aside to dry completely.

3. Tie in fine tan or white thread at bend of hook. Select a good quality hackle of dark chocolate brown, with barbules no longer than twice the hook's gap, and strip off webby lower barbs. Bind by stem to hook, on edge, perpendicular to shank, with glossy side toward eye.

4. Wind hackle and tie off with half-hitch. Wax a short length of the tying thread next to the hook and apply a dubbing of ruddy brown fur. Wind dubbing forward for body and half-hitch thread well behind eye. Select a second hackle similar to first and bind at forward end of body, with glossy side facing bend. Wind front hackle and tie off with half-hitch.

5. Cut a wide "V" from the top of the wound hackles.

6. By now your wing should be dry. Remove it from hackle plier and hold in right hand by tips of inverted barbules. Manipulating thread with left hand, tie in wing in flat position by barbs only, next to end of center rib. Make a few extra turns of thread and half-hitch. Then trim off unused hackle tip as shown.

7. Finally, whip finish thread at head and coat head with black lacquer. Then trim a "V" from undersides of hackles. This completes Little Black Stonefly.

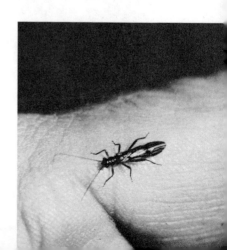

8. A little black stonefly—the natural.

The Michigan Stone

If it were possible to catalog all the dry fly patterns in use in the United States today the total number would stagger the imagination. In addition to the countless standard patterns which originated in this country there are still a number in common use which came from England, where the dry fly was born. Then there are the many local patterns tailored to fit specific needs in certain areas but seldom well known beyond the boundaries of their origins.

Most dry fly patterns are aimed at representing mayflies, although limited attention has been accorded the caddis, and a long overdue recognition of midges and the terrestrial insects has been under way. The lowly stonefly seems to be the unglamorous, poor cousin of the insect world, at least in the eyes of many dry fly anglers. Exceptions are a few large western patterns like the Sofa Pillow, which represent the huge stoneflies known in the West as Salmon Flies. True, there are a few Yellow Sally patterns around, both wet and dry, but most of them allude to the little stoneflies in color only, holding more closely to the mayfly in form.

Yellow Sally is the common name of the little yellow stonefly, *Isoperla bilineata* (and other related species). The name originated in the British Isles, where separate species of *Isoperla* are abundant. Also included among the Yellow Sallys are smaller stoneflies with a distinct greenish cast which belong to the genera *Alloperla* and *Chloroperla*. Typical of stoneflies, the Yellow Sally

Isoperla bilineata

nymph crawls out of the water and emergence of the adult takes place on rocks, logs or any convenient air-exposed object. Emergence offers little opportunity for a rise of trout except on windy days, when a few adults may be blown onto the water. Following emergence these shy creatures hide under rocks at streamside, on the shaded side of tree trunks, or in foliage where they are well camouflaged. However, when the females are ready to lay their eggs they appear over the water in great numbers and it is at this time that their value to the dry fly fisherman becomes evident.

Anglers who ply the rock-bottomed streams of Pennsylvania's Northern Tier counties are familiar with the ovipositing swarms of Yellow Sallys which appear over the riffles on warm June and July evenings. She's a pretty insect, graceful and unhurried in flight, and when she dips down to the water to lay her eggs she is equally attractive to the trout.

The Michigan Stone is a dry fly pattern originated by the late Paul Young, famed rod builder and fly dresser from Detroit. We first learned of the pattern some years ago while fishing the Au Sable River with Mr. Young and his wife, Martha. We were so impressed by its effectiveness when *Isoperla* was over the water that we brought it back to try on Pennsylvania waters. Here it has proved a valuable fly, not only during the flights of Yellow Sally but as a general attractor fly as well. Recently while in England my wife, Marion, had a rare opportunity to fish some of the famed British chalk streams and there she found the brown trout just as receptive to the Michigan Stone as they are at home.

The original pattern was tied, as it is now, with hackles fore and aft to eliminate the need for tail support. The wings, tied flat over the body to represent the wing posture of the natural, were made from the fine-textured hair of the dik-dik, the tiny African antelope. However, dik-dik hair is difficult to come by these days, as is the hair of its closest substitute, the Asiatic mouse deer, so in tying the Michigan Stone shown in the photographs we are going to use the speckled tips of the thinnest natural deer body hair for wings. Since the pattern covers several species included in the Yellow Sally group it's good practice to tie it in sizes #16 and #18, some with yellow bodies and others with chartreuse. Another variation, to represent the greenish *Alloperla*, is tied in size #20 with chartreuse body and yellowish-olive hackles.

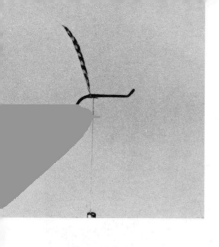

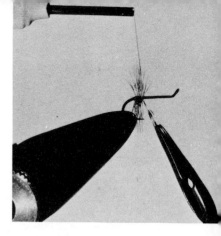

1. Clamp a fine wire, size #16 hook in the vise and tie in fine yellow tying thread at bend. Select a grizzly hackle of good quality, with barbules no longer than twice the hook gap. Strip away the webby lower portion and bind hackle to hook at bend. Position hackle at right angle to hook with edge of hackle facing tyer and with glossy side facing eye of hook. Then bend hackle root forward and bind with three turns.

2. Attach hackle pliers to hackle tip and wind forward in close turns. Bind down tip of hackle with two turns and half-hitch. Trim off excess hackle tip.

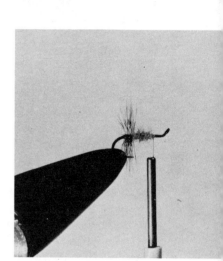

3. Wax 2 or 3 inches of the thread next to the hook and apply a moderately thin dubbing of yellow or chartreuse-dyed kapok (or rabbit fur) by rolling it around thread with fingers.

4. Wind dubbing forward to form body, allowing ample space in front for wings and hackle. Body should not be tapered.

5. Clip a small bunch (thickness of a kitchen match) of fine-textured deer body hair from hide. Pull out short hairs and even up the tips. Lay hair flat over body with tips extending slightly beyond bend and bind hair in front of body with several turns. Half-hitch. Trim off excess butts to a bevel, as shown.

6. Select another grizzly hackle with slightly shorter barbules than the first. Tie in as in photograph 1, over wing butts, but this time with dull side facing eye. Then attach hackle pliers and wind hackle as in photograph 2.

7. After the wound hackle is tied off and the excess tips trimmed, build a neat head with thread and whip finish. Apply a drop of head lacquer to head.

8. Michigan Stones: *Isoperla* version above; *Alloperla* variation below.

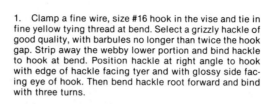
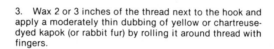
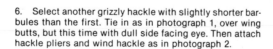

The Egg-Laying Stonefly

On some of the large trout streams in the West the major dry fly excitement is caused by the so-called Salmon Fly or Willow Fly hatches. These are flights of enormous stoneflies, some of which measure two inches or more in length. When they are on the water some of the largest trout in the stream surface-feed with a fury seldom seen when mayflies are on the water.

The big stoneflies belong to the genus *Pteronarcys* and although they are best known to fishermen in the West they are also present on many of our eastern streams. In the East their common habitat is in slower water than that commonly associated with the flat stonefly nymphs of *perla* and *Acroneuria*, both of which prefer fast, well-aerated water. *Pteronarcys* nymphs like the cold, clear headwaters of upland spring brooks, and their principal diet is decaying vegetation. They can often be found on the upstream side of submerged logs, where silt and debris collect. The nymphs are very dark in coloration and robust, lacking the flatness so characteristic of the riffle-dwelling nymphs. They are often called Curlers because of their habit of rolling up into a ball when disturbed.

Like most stoneflies, the adults of *Pteronarcys* offer scant opportunity for dry fly fishing on emergence. But the return of the females to lay their eggs on the water is quite another matter for their method of ovipositing creates a disturbance too great to be overlooked by large trout. The big females release their eggs while swimming across and upstream, wildly fluttering their outstretched wings and leaving a "V"-wake behind. The response by a big trout to such a performance is often a crashing, shattering rise, the likes of which can leave the bystanding angler in a trembling state of anticipation.

From an angling standpoint the presence of flies as large as *Pteronarcys* can only be significant when large trout are present in the stream and are willing to feed upon the big insects. This would appear to negate the sporting possibilities of these flies on the little headwater mountain brooks, where small brook trout are the principal occupants. Fortunately, however, *Pteronarcys* also appears in good numbers on some of our large, spring-fed streams which contain big brown trout. Penn's Creek gets a good showing of the giant stoneflies around mid-June, and knowledgeable anglers are well-acquainted with them. They were once plentiful on the East Branch of the Delaware River in New York but it is reported that ecological changes have brought about their near-extinction on that watershed.

Unlike its western cousins, whose egg-laying flights occur during daylight hours, the *Pteronarcys* of the

Pteronarcys, the giant stonefly

East is mainly nocturnal. There are occasional exceptions, when it appears in late afternoon on dark, overcast days, but most of the fishing to the giant stoneflies is the domain of the night fishermen, on streams where night fishing is permitted.

The Egg-Laying Stonefly pattern is a dry fly made almost entirely of hollow deer body hair. It is designed for maximum flotation, necessarily so because it must be agitated to simulate the fluttering commotion made by the ovipositing females. Although stoneflies are four-winged insects the two flared hair wings of the artificial are sufficient to simulate the spread-wing posture of the natural fly on the water. As a night fly the pattern should be tied in sizes #6 to #10, on long-shank hooks. Mustad's #94832, with its 2X long shank and 2X fine wire, is a good hook for this purpose. As in most night fishing, the leader should be stouter than those normally used in daylight for the rise of a large trout is often much more forceful under cover of darkness.

In addition to fishing the Egg-Laying Stonefly when the giant *Pteronarcys* is on the water, there is a secondary use of the pattern which permits daytime fishing. Late in the regular trout season and on warm days during the extended fall season the big, fully matured grasshoppers are active. When they get on the water they often flail the surface with their wings and float with wings extended. Then a size #10 Egg-Laying Stonefly becomes a 'hopper imitation. With it I have caught some fine autumn trout. Meadow streams are particularly good prospects for this kind of fishing but even the mountain trout of the woodland streams seem to know about grasshoppers by season's end.

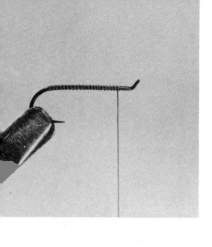

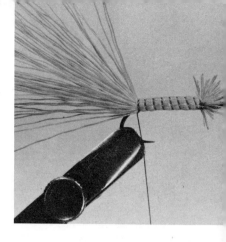

TYING THE EGG-LAYING STONEFLY

1. Clamp a long shank, fine wire hook in vise. (Size #10 shown.) Tie in size A orange Nymo thread behind eye and spiral thread to bend, then spiral thread forward and half-hitch behind eye.

2. Cut a bunch of yellow-dyed deer body hair from the hide (bunch should be about ¼ inch wide when flattened) and comb out the short hairs and fuzz. Hold hair length-wise on top of hook with butts extending over eye. Make two tight turns of thread around hair and hook behind eye and spiral thread in spaced turns to bend of hook. Half-hitch.

3. For tails select two short quill fibres from a gray mallard primary and bind to sides with two turns. Then fold quill butts back and wind over with two turns to lock tails in place. Trim waste quill butts as shown.

4. Pull the unbound hair forward over the back of the sub-body and spiral thread forward in spaced turns. Half-hitch in position shown.

5. For wings cut a ¼-inch bunch of natural brown deer body hair and bind behind head over body. Half-hitch. Wings should be 1½ times the length of hook. Rough-trim the head to get the long hair butts out of the way.

6. Separate the hair wing into two halves and position at forty-five degree angles by crisscrossing thread in figure-eight turns. Then pass thread under head and whip-finish behind eye, as shown. Cut off waste thread and lacquer finish windings.

7. Place a drop of lacquer at the base of each wing. When nearly dry, squeeze with tweezers to flatten wings. Finally, finish-trim the head.

8. Finished Egg-Laying Stonefly.

63

An Early Black Caddis

Coinciding with the burst of wildflowers in spring is the appearance of small, dark caddisflies over our trout streams. A scant quarter-inch in length and sooty-black, these little Trichopterans seem to thrive on sunlight, for like the blossoming flora, they are at their best on bright days. Their emergence generally begins in the latter part of April and extends to late May or early June, with a few stragglers appearing until mid-July.

The Early Black Caddis most common to trout water in the eastern United States is known by entomologists as *Chimarrha aterrima*. The larvae are fast water inhabitants which do not build cases but instead spin cylindrical nets of fine mesh, woven from the most delicate silken threads. The nets resemble the fingers of a glove. Several are often found together on the underside of rocks. The upstream end of the net is open, by means of which particles of food are trapped. On the opposite end is a small opening, through which the larva can escape if danger threatens. During the pupal stage the insect resides in a case of stones.

Completed Early Black Caddis

Although the Early Black Caddis is traditionally represented by a wet fly, I have found it advantageous to interpret it with a floater because of its frequent appearance during the prime dry fly time of late May. The pattern is a low-floating fly with tent-shaped downwings. Front-to-rear hackling is employed, mainly because winding the hackles rearward over the tapered body points the barbules slightly forward in front and backward in the rear, all of which promotes better balance on the water and more closely resembles the posture of the insect's legs. Winding the tying thread back through the wound hackles to the head of the fly may be accomplished without depressing the barbules and thus bound, the palmered hackles are fixed to the fly in a most enduring way.

Several aspects of the winging method should be noted. The quill section is coated with thin vinyl cement for durability but the thin tip—the end of the quill section to be secured to the hook—is left untreated. Then, after folding the wing to achieve the roof-like shape, it is bound to the hook by holding the tip with the right hand and making the initial turns of thread with the left. The thread binding should only be over the uncoated tip of the quill. This procedure simplifies the winging and prevents disturbing the hackles, as would be the case if the left hand held the wing in position. The diagonal trimming of the folded wing achieves the characteristic notch at the rear of the caddis wings, visible when viewed from the underside.

Entomologists generally use the terms sedges and caddisflies interchangeably in reference to the insects of the order Trichoptera. Interestingly, David Jacques, the eminent British angler-entomologist, makes a distinction between the two, contending that although all Trichoptera are sedges, technically, only the case-builders are caddisflies. That *C. aterrima* should properly be called the Early Black Sedge is a matter of purely academic interest to anglers, and I'm sure, of no consequence to the trout. They simply take them as they come; caddis or sedge, fish treat them as a gourmet delight.

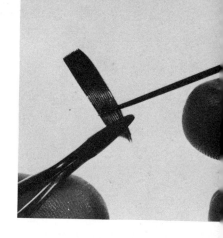

TYING THE EARLY BLACK CADDIS

1.   Clamp a size #18, fine wire hook in the vise and bind tying thread to shank behind eye, allowing ample space to attach wing. Then select one each black and chocolate brown hackles of dry fly quality, with barbules about twice as long as gap of hook. Remove webby portion and bind to shank in a vertical position with glossy sides facing bend and edges facing tyer. Bend hackle roots forward and bind with several turns, as shown. Trim off excess roots.

2.   For wing, cut a section of black-dyed duck wing quill about 3/16 inch wide and stroke the fibres until it is straight. Grasp the thin end of quill with hackle pliers and coat the rest of the quill on its shiny side with vinyl cement. Put aside to dry.

3.   Wax a short length of the tying thread next to the hook and apply a thin dubbing of black kapok or spun fur. Then wind the dubbed thread rearward, forming a tapered body, to the bend and half-hitch.

4.   Wind the hackles separately, taking a full turn in front, then spiralling back to bend in open palmer fashion and tying off each at rear of body. Half-hitch.

5.   With fine-pointed scissors trim off the hackle both above and below the body, leaving only those barbules extending from the sides.

6.   (Top view) Carefully wind the tying thread forward in spaced turns through the wound hackle and half-hitch at fore end of body.

7.   Remove the quill wing prepared in step 2 from the hackle pliers and fold it along its length, with the dull side of the quill inside. Then grasp the thin tip of the quill (the untreated part) with the right hand and hold it in position while binding it to hook with the left hand. Trim away waste, build neat head with thread, whip-finish, and cut off excess thread.

8.   Holding scissors at an angle, trim wing to size by making a diagonal cut, as shown. Approximately ¼ the length of wing should extend behind bend of hook. After applying cement to the head and to the hackle tie-off in rear, the Early Black Caddis is completed.

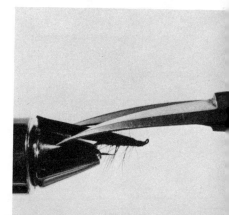

A Parachute Sedge

We have previously noted that in the order Trichoptera the British make a distinction between caddisflies, which build larval cases, and sedges, which do not. American entomologists make no such differentiation between the two, preferring to channel all Trichopterans into the single designation of caddisflies. Of course, entomologists are concerned only with the insects' scientific names, and descriptive common names assigned by fishermen often overlap several species and generally are applied only to flies of value from an angling standpoint. This is fortunate; in the North American continent there are more than 600 species of Trichoptera and if common names were allotted to all, I'm sure total confusion would prevail.

Despite the unreliability of common names in the vast entomology of our country, I think it is of value to the fly dresser, if not the entomologist, to categorize Trichopterans as either sedges or caddisflies. The tyer is generally interested in representing the significant forms in any given insect's life cycle, and the applicable designation of sedge or caddis would indicate whether the larval form is a "naked nymph" or cased larva.

In recent years caddisflies have received more than customary attention from fly fishermen. It is said that Trichopterans can survive in water too polluted for the more delicate mayflies and stoneflies; thus, they are the insects of the future, at least as far as meaningful fishing hatches are concerned. It is a sad commentary on the deterioration of water quality in certain areas. Yet, in relatively pure streams where a variety of insects flourish, the Trichopterans receive their share of attention from trout, often in preference to more exotic forms.

Spring generally brings on some exceptional hatches of sedges and caddis in western Pennsylvania. On the Fish-For-Fun water of Slippery Rock Creek there is usually a continuous three-week period of this activity in May that furnishes excellent fishing. Several species are represented but the dominant hatch is a tannish little sedge of the genus *Hydropsyche* which is on the water several hours each day when conditions are favorable.

Like *Chimarrha*, the larvae of *Hydropsyche* build finely woven nets. Those of the latter are funnel-shaped and attached to rocks in swift water, opening upstream. At the rear of the net is a shelter of tiny pebbles or vegetable matter, to which the larva can retreat. The net not only assists in camouflaging the larva's residence but it serves as a food catcher as well.

Recently, the excellent hatch on Slippery Rock Creek gave me an opportunity to experiment with a new sedge dry fly pattern, born of the current hackle shortage. Previously I had tied the tent-wing flies with open-palmer hackle, clipped above and below, and they worked well, indeed. But even the sparsest of palmering requires two hackles and I discovered that my irreplaceable prime hackle was diminishing at an alarming rate. The solution was a sedge with the hackle dressed parachute-style, which uses a single hackle most efficiently. The hackle is wound around a nylon anchor above the thorax in the same manner as in several spent spinner patterns we have previously described.

Not only did the Parachute Sedge float as well as the previous palmer dressing, it presented practically the same light pattern on the surface film and was equally effective. Also, on days when the trout were taking the naturals as they skittered across current, I found that the flat, parachute hackle permitted activating the fly without dunking. Although the Parachute Sedge described here was intended to represent the little *Hydropsyche*, the general design lends itself to any caddis type, with appropriate changes in size and color.

Completed Parachute Sedge

66

TYING A PARACHUTE SEDGE

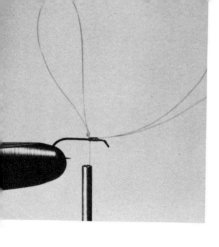

1. Clamp a size #16 dry fly hook in vise and bind yellow tying thread to shank well behind eye. Double a 6-inch strand of 4X monofilament and form a loop by knotting the doubled monofil. Bind loop to top of shank as shown. Allow about 1/16 inch between knot and shank.

2. Trim off excess ends of monofilament. Then spiral thread back to bend and wax about 2 inches of thread next to shank. Apply a dubbing of tan fur or synthetic to waxed thread.

3. Roll fur around thread with fingertips and wind dubbing forward to form a tapered abdomen, ending at monofil. Select a light ginger hackle with barbule length about twice the hook gap. Strip off lower webby barbs and bind stem to shank, as shown, with glossy side of hackle facing downward. Trim excess hackle stem.

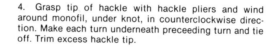

4. Grasp tip of hackle with hackle pliers and wind around monofil, under knot, in counterclockwise direction. Make each turn underneath preceeding turn and tie off. Trim excess hackle tip.

5. Pull nylon loop forward and down, straddling shank and pressing front barbules back. Then tie off monofil and cut off excess.

6. Apply a little more dubbing to thread and form thorax in front of hackle. Tie off, allowing space for winging behind eye.

7. For wings, cut a single section of light turkey quill about ¼ inch wide. Hold tip with hackle pliers and coat all but tip with vinyl cement or acrylic lacquer.

8. Fold quill section along its length and tie in by its uncoated tip. Wing should be tent-shaped, extending back over body. Trim end of wing at angle, as shown, to create rear notch. Whip finish behind eye and lacquer head.

Minutiae of the Order Diptera

Sometimes finding the solution is easier than recognizing the problem. On many streams we had observed the swarms of tiny gnats over the water, flying in a curious figure-eight pattern. Occasionally a trout would fling itself full length out of the water, apparently attempting to pick the little insects out of the air. This was disconcerting because I knew of no way to deliver a fly in such a fashion. So I chose to ignore the phenomenon, regarding it as inopportune, at least from an angling standpoint. Then one August afternoon in Michigan, when we were fishing the South Branch of the Au Sable River, I discovered that the little gnats of Hilara, sometimes called dance flies, do indeed have a place in the fly fisher's scheme.

My wife and I were fishing above Chase Bridge when a large mating swarm of *Hilara* appeared upstream over the water. Soon conspicuous black specks began to appear on the water just downstream of the swarm and invariably they were taken by trout. With insect net in hand I waded out to intercept several of the drifting specks and found they were mating pairs of gnats. The Fore-and-Aft Gnat is a dry fly pattern born of that revelation on the Au Sable. It has become a consistent producer when fallen mating pairs are on the water, but it is important that the angler station himself well downstream from the swarms because it is here that the pairs are taken by trout.

Midge hatches are common on nearly all trout water. The occurrence of several species may overlap, particularly in late afternoon and evening. As neither gnats nor midges have tails, patterns representing them should balance on the surface without requiring tail support. Actually, the Fore-and-Aft Gnat works well as a midge pattern, too, and with variations in body coloration it serves as an auxiliary to the Straddle-Legged Midge when Chironomids are on the water.

The long-legged, mosquito-like midges are remarkably adaptable insects. Blood worms, the familiar red midge larvae, are so colored because their bloodstream contains hemoglobin. Hemoglobin absorbs oxygen which is stored by the insects for later use as required, enabling them to live in water with low oxygen content. Although blood worms flourish in clean streams, when they are found in streams to the exclusion of other common aquatic insects it it an indication that the water is likely polluted.

A Fore-and-Aft Gnat

The tiny two-winged flies of the order Diptera play an important role in the diet of trout. Their great availability as larvae, pupae, and adults quantitatively compensates for their small size and trout eat them in surprising numbers. Midges, the mosquito-like Chironomids, are well known to all anglers, but equally important are the small Black Gnats of the genus *Hilara*. The latter appear over much of the season in huge swarms, flying erratically a few inches above the water. In slow-moving pools trout are frequently tempted to leap clear of the surface to intercept the tiny insects.

The swarms of *Hilara* are evidently related to mating. The individual insects within the swarms may be seen flying back and forth in an abbreviated zig-zag pattern, always alert to any small insect or bit of debris floating with the current. Occasionally one of the little gnats will dart down and pick a small, floating insect off the water. The prey is usually a midge, which is wrapped in a silken gauze spun by the male gnat and presented by him to his bride-to-be as a wedding gift. Many of the mating pairs get on the water and are taken by trout, providing a real opportunity for the fly fisherman.

The Fore-and-Aft Gnat pattern shown in the illustrations was originally tied as a dry fly representation of the mating *Hilara*, and has proved its worth many times, not only when *Hilara* were extant but as a general midge pattern as well. Generally trout take the drifting gnats and midges in a quiet rise form and it's not always easy to ascertain the size of the rising fish unless it can be seen.

On a favorite limestone meadow stream in south-central Pennsylvania there is a short, smooth-water stretch with a high bank on one side. The bank is covered with wild rose bushes which extend down to the water, creating an overhang of several feet in depth, under which the brown trout like to hide. I came to learn that, even when no fish were showing, if I crept up to the edge of the opposite bank and quietly seated myself behind a tuft of tall grass, I didn't have long to wait before a trout or two would move out into feeding position. One day I caught and returned a trout of perhaps eleven

inches, taken from a pocket against the watercress just below the rose bushes. The next morning I returned and found what I assumed to be the same trout rising in the little pocket. Since no flies were visible on the water I guessed the trout was midging and accordingly bent on a #22 Fore-and-Aft Gnat. The first float was met with the familiar soft rise but when I tightened a fine brown trout of some eighteen inches came cartwheeling out of the water. With a screech of the reel he tore upstream, crossed over under a bed of watercress, and fouled the frail tippet on a snag under the bushy overhang.

Most fishermen change to a different pattern of fly when a trout is raised and missed because the original pattern is often refused when it is offered a second time. I've had considerable success with the little Fore-and-Aft Gnat as a back up pattern after missing a rise, particularly when there is no specific hatch on the water.

The pattern is as simple as possible and is extremely easy to tie. There are no tails (because real gnats have none) and the fly balances perfectly on its two hackles. I have long been partial to black-dyed kapok dubbed on the tying thread as body material but any fine-textured black fur may be substituted. The correct hackle is medium dun gray, preferably with that elusive, sparkling translucency so difficult to find these days. I also tie an alternate version with grizzly hackles because it's a little easier to see on the water in poor light. Whichever hackle is used, the barbules should not be longer than twice the gap of the hook. I use the pattern in sizes #20 through #24 and find the smallest sizes to be most effective on slow pools and glassy, smooth-topped runs.

As a final note I would like to recommend the use of barbless hooks, particularly to the ever-increasing number of anglers who share the philosophy of catch and release. The barbs of most small hooks are out of proportion to the overall size, making it difficult to extricate the fly without damage to the trout and/or the fly itself. This is especially true when the hook is lodged in the tough maxillary. It's a simple matter to squeeze down the barb with pliers or tweezers prior to dressing the fly.

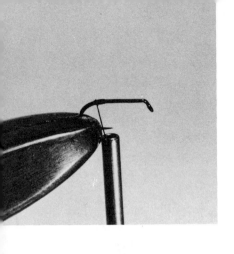

TYING A FORE-AND-AFT GNAT

1.   Clamp a small hook (size #20 to #24) in the vise and bind fine black thread at bend.

2.   Select a medium dun gray hackle with barbules no longer than twice the gap of the hook. Strip away the webby lower portion and bind the stem to the hook so that the hackle stands at right angle and the glossy side faces the eye of the hook. Bend root forward and bind along shank. Trim excess root as shown.

3.   Grip the hackle's tip in hackle pliers and wind forward in close turns. Tie off with two turns of thread and half-hitch. Trim waste hackle tip.

4.   Apply tacky wax or varnish to about 1 inch of the thread next to the hook. Roll a dubbing of black kapok (or any fine-textured black fur) around waxed thread with fingertips.

5.   Wind dubbing forward 2/3 the length of shank and half-hitch thread.

6.   Select another hackle and repeat step 2, this time facing the glossy side toward the bend.

7.   Wind front hackle forward and tie off, leaving space for head in back of eye. Trim waste hackle tip, then make a neat head with thread and whip finish. A drop of head lacquer completes fly.

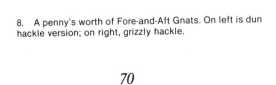

8.   A penny's worth of Fore-and-Aft Gnats. On left is dun hackle version; on right, grizzly hackle.

The Straddle-Legged Midge

George La Branche advocated simulating a hatch, when trout were not rising, by repetitive casting of the same dry fly over a known or suspected lie. But when trout, and especially browns, are tipping up rhythmically to take midges, the angler can fall victim to the law of diminishing returns by repeatedly casting the same fly over the same fish. This is particularly true if the trout has risen and been missed or if he has been scratched. Often the trout will go right on feeding to the naturals and he'll still look closely at, but refuse, the artificial that was snatched away from him. Then, generally, he becomes less and less interested in it until eventually he disregards it entirely.

Familiarity breeds contempt. I doubt that trout have read this old adage, but somehow its message has penetrated into their behavior. In any small-fly fishing it pays to have a backup pattern to change to when the going gets really tough. When midges are on the water in quantity they are often of mixed variety and sometimes changing to a pattern of different color or form, providing the small size is retained, is enough to gain fresh attention.

Midges, the Chironomids, are often referred to as "non-biting mosquitos" because of their resemblance to the long-legged pests. *Chironomus lobiferus*, the black midge and *C. modestus*, the green midge are common to Pennsylvania's trout streams and both are deserving of representative dry fly patterns. The Straddle-Legged Midge is the result of an attempt to come up with a spare pattern for *C. lobiferus* with a slight variation in form. This is achieved with the use of outrigger hackle barbules to represent the long trailing legs, a dominant feature of the naturals. These not only balance the fly perfectly on the water but give a more accurate light pattern than the prevalent use of tails, of which real midges have none. Although the pattern illustrated represents the black midge, the same style of dressing may be utilized in many color variations. For the green midge, only the substitution of greenish olive body dubbing need be made. Optionally, medium dun hackle may be used (and probably it more accurately represents the wings and legs) but grizzly seems to be equally effective and is a bit easier to see in failing light.

At the risk of being branded an heretic, I would like to suggest at least a partial solution to the growing scarcity of good hackle for small flies. These are unusual times, when prime necks are not only difficult to find but are bringing nightmarish prices. The classic formula of hackle size, except for spiders and variants, dictates that the barbules be no longer than 1½ to 2 times the gap of the hook. Even when one is fortunate enough to find and afford a neck with all the requisites for good dry flies, the small hackles, those that qualify for #20s to #24s (and smaller, according to the formula) are relatively few in number at best. Although it has been frowned upon in the past by some, I don't believe that trimming slightly oversized hackle down to size should today be considered a cardinal sin. There are benefits to be gained by trimming a size #18 hackle down to size #20—or a size #20 to #22 or #24. The larger hackle feather has a stronger rib and its greater length permits the tyer to eliminate all the webby barbules and use only the upper, webfree portion, making for better floatability. Perhaps the untrimmed points of the barbules give the appearance of greater delicacy, but it is an illusion based more on tradition than practical consideration. Look closely at any insect, large or small, and you'll see that its feet, the points of contact with the surface film, are blunt, not pointed. This is not meant to condemn using hackle of appropriate size if one has it. But beginning fly tyers should not shy away from dressing small flies merely because they lack hackle of traditional dimensions.

Midging the Fish-For-Fun water at Slippery Rock Creek

TYING THE
STRADDLE-LEGGED MIDGE

1.   Clamp a dry fly hook (size #20 to #24) in vise and bind fine black thread to shank behind eye. For ribbing, tie in a 5-inch strand of yellow thread and wind tying thread over it back to bend.

2.   Wax about 2 inches of the tying thread next to the shank and apply a thin dubbing of black kapok or any fine-textured black fur. Wind dubbing forward to form a tapered body and half-hitch about 1/8 inch behind eye.

3.   Wind the ribbing thread in spaced turns, counterclockwise, and tie off at fore end of body. Cut off excess ribbing thread.

4.   (Top view) For rear legs, tie in two grizzly hackle barbules together atop the thorax position, angling the tips away and slightly downward. Then tie in two more barbules, angling these toward you and matching the downward slope of the first two.

5.   Select a grizzly hackle with barbules no longer than 1½ to 2 times the hook gap. Remove the web near the base and bind the stem to hook with hackle at right angle, on edge, with glossy side facing bend. (Note: Slightly oversized hackle may be used and trimmed to size.)

6.   (Top view) Wind the hackle, tie off and trim excess tip. Then build a neat head and whip finish. Trim off thread and coat head with lacquer. This completes the Straddle-Legged Midge.

The Speckled Midge

If one were to be terribly fussy about it, the word "midge" should be restricted to suggest the little aquatic Diptera (and some are not all that small) of the family Chironomidae, as well as those of several subfamilies. But fly fishermen tend to expand the meaning to include the broad spectrum of true midges, gnats, and diverse minutiae, both aquatic and terrestrial, ever-present in the water's surface film. And, it's not a bad rationale at all, although entomologists tend to become upset about such plebeian inaccuracies. Personally, I like the anglers' designation because the word is descriptive of the size. Besides, my flyboxes are crowded enough already and if I had to categorize the little flies into separate designations (and compartments) my vest would have to sprout a few more pockets.

There are times when trout become selective to specific midges, particularly during evening hatches, but the midge-feeders of midday seem to be more catholic in their tastes and willing to sample the sundry available to them at that time.

I can never have too many midge patterns. Spents, fore-and-afts, skaters, straddle-legs, in a range of sizes and colors, all serve a purpose. The incessant, midge-feeding trout is one of angling's finest challenges and if one stays with an individual fish until the war of nerves is won (or lost), the chances are the angler has gone through a variety of patterns, particularly if he failed to hook the trout on one of the first few casts. After the trout is raised and missed the law of diminishing returns sets in and the effectiveness of a given pattern declines rapidly. Then the angler must choose between resting the trout, moving on to find another midge-feeder, or changing to a new pattern. I prefer the last choice because I enjoy nothing more than working over a difficult trout until I either catch him or put him down. Of course, failures often balance out the successes, and from the standpoint of tallying sheer numbers of trout caught I would be better advised to seek out fresh, unpestered fish. But if I'm fortunate enough to be successful, the satisfaction is far greater than in catching several random fish and the additional time spent is worthwhile.

The Speckled Midge doesn't represent a specific insect but it has often worked wonders as a backup pattern, after a more conventional midge was missed or refused. The form and light pattern offer a variation from the norm and sometimes a slight contrast gives just the edge required. Palmered dry flies are sometimes called "buzz" patterns and it is speculated that they represent insects with their wings vibrating. The Speckled Midge is hackled open palmer, with the hackles tied in at the head posi-

Completed Speckled Midge

tion, dull sides facing forward, and wound individually back to the bend in spaced turns. This method utilizes the convex profile of the hackles to position the barbules in the approximate posture of the insect's legs on the water, flared forward in front and rearward in back. This also provides the fly with maximum floating stability.

Olive tying thread serves a two-fold purpose: to bind and tie off the hackles and to provide a body for the pattern. A whip finish at the rear of the fly, behind the hackle, may sound a bit intimidating at first but if you can make a whip finish by hand at the head of a fly you'll have no trouble. However, a whip-finishing tool cannot be used here without crushing the hackle and if you are dependent on the tool for this function you may substitute several half-hitches.

The Speckled Midge derives its name from the flecked appearance of the grizzly-brown hackle mix—the reliable Adams hackle combination—and its peppery image makes it easy to see in poor light. Useful sizes are #20 to #24. Don't be discouraged if you haven't hackle of proper size for the smaller hooks. Simply tie the fly slightly oversized and trim the hackle evenly until the barbs are no longer than 1½ to 2 times the hook's gap. Trimmed flies are perhaps not as aesthetically pleasing but they don't suffer one whit in effectiveness, I can assure you.

TYING THE SPECKLED MIDGE

1.   Clamp a dry fly hook (#20 to #24) in vise and tie in olive tying thread at bend, opposite barb. Wind thread forward to eye in close turns, then back from eye about four turns. Half-hitch or allow thread to hang under weight.

2.   Select one each brown and grizzly hackles with barbules 1½ to 2 times as long as the hook's gap. (See text for alternative.) Remove the webby lower barbules and place hackles together. Tie in perpendicular to shank, with glossy sides facing bend. After securing with figure-eight turns, bend stems back along shank and bind. Trim excess stems.

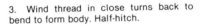

3.   Wind thread in close turns back to bend to form body. Half-hitch.

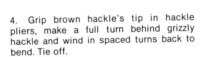

4.   Grip brown hackle's tip in hackle pliers, make a full turn behind grizzly hackle and wind in spaced turns back to bend. Tie off.

5.   Then wind the grizzly hackle, following the path of the brown hackle, and tie off at bend. Trim waste hackle tips.

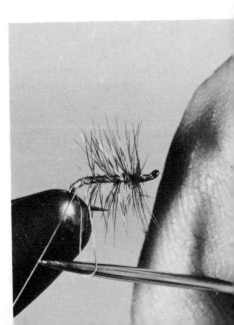

6.   Make a manual whip finish at bend behind hackle and cut off thread. Apply a drop of head lacquer to finish windings.

74

Terrestrial Insects
and a Maverick Pattern

Not too many years ago fly fishermen typically put away their trout gear after the major mayfly hatches had ended, turning to bass fishing, golf, or other outdoor sports to fill the void in summer activity. That is no longer the case. Pioneered by Crowe, Marinaro, and Fox and nurtured by the likes of Schwiebert, Almy, and others, angling to the land insects is now recognized as an important contributor to the fly fisherman's season-long success. On streams where aquatic insects are found wanting, the terrestrials are prime stimulators of surface-feeding activity.

There is virtually no end to the list of terrestrial insects which become water-bound. Although their incidence on the water is accidental, the frequency of its occurrence makes trout cognizant of them. They are particularly plentiful on meadow streams; one needs only to walk through the tall grass of a typical meadow to be aware of the enormous quantity and variety of land insects found there, from the largest of grasshoppers to the tiniest of leafhoppers. Many seasoned anglers contend that the opportunities of catching really large trout are greater during grasshopper season than during the famous Green Drake hatches. Crickets, too, attract big trout, as do beetles and ants when they are on the water in quantity. Terrestrial patterns may, to us, lack the visual beauty of traditional dry flies, but trout apparently have their own sense of aesthetics.

It is said that Halford discontinued fishing the Hare's Ear because he could not reconcile why trout took it so consistently. Hoagy's Little Orange Mayfly fits roughly into that category. Whether trout take it for a baitfish, larva, or purely out of curiosity is a moot point. The fact is, they take it and I have witnessed its effectiveness in the most unlikely of situations.

The Quill-Back Beetle

One of the important terrestrial insects deserving of dry fly representation is the beetle, for there are more than a quarter-million beetle species in the world and over 28,000 species in the North American continent. Most beetles are terrestrial insects but they occur in such numbers that it is inevitable that many get into the water and are eaten by trout. The characteristic low-riding posture of the insect, floating flush in the surface film, makes it difficult to see except at close range.

Several years ago my wife and I were fishing Dunbar and had paused for lunch at streamside when Bill Workman arrived on the scene. Bill had been fishing since early morning on one of Dunbar's cold tributaries, high up the mountain, and he showed us a beautiful wild brown trout he had caught there. Curious to see what the trout had been busily feeding on, Bill performed an autopsy and we could scarcely believe our eyes. In the stomach was a huge mass of beetles and nothing else. They were a wide variety of sizes, from tiny indigo beetles to large ground beetles about three-fourths of an inch long. We estimated that the trout had taken upwards of 200 beetles for his morning meal. It was the most outstanding example of single-minded feeding I have ever seen. Even more remarkable was the availability of so many beetles to a single trout, feeding within a limited range, in what must have been a relatively short time.

Dry fly fishermen can thank three Pennsylvanians for pioneering in the field of beetle fishing. Following the infestation of the Japanese beetle in the Cumberland Valley, Charles Fox and Vincent Marinaro were studying the increased surface-feeding activity of the trout in the LeTort. Early in the 1940s Fox devised a pattern made by cementing a wingless wet fly to a slotted coffee bean. At the same time Marinaro developed the now classic LeTort Beetle, made with open palmer hackle clipped above and below the hook and one or two large jungle cock nails tied flat to represent the oval body. Meanwhile John Crowe, fishing the woodland streams of northwestern Pennsylvania, fashioned an effective pattern made by binding a bunch of deer hair at the hook's bend, pulling it over the back and tying off the hair behind the eye, allowing a few hairs to remain at the sides and in front to represent legs and antennae.

My own entry to the short ledger of beetle patterns is offered because of its adaptability to many beetle types and because it embodies an unusual technique in manipulating deer hair. Although the Quill-Back Beetle shown in the photographs represents the black ground beetle, there is an infinite variety of color combinations possible by varying the color of the hair body and of the quill back. In addition to black beetles there are many common species with yellow bodies and black wings, orange bodies with gray wings, and still others as iridescent blue or green overall. The shape of beetles varies with species, too; some are broadly oval while others have parallel sides, features easily simulated in the imitation by varying the density of the hair. Generally, though, the flat, ovoid shape is most desirable and this is achieved with a minimum of hair. The secret lies in dividing the central bundle of hair into two bunches, then twisting each bunch as it is positioned along its respective side of the hook. Twisting the hair makes it firm and manageable, preventing individual hairs from slipping under the body. Then with the aid of vinyl cement the quill sections are moulded over the hair body and the whole is a lightweight, durable, sure-floating fly.

For general use I prefer the Quill-Back Beetle in sizes #14 and #16 but there are many occasions when tiny ones down to #22s are needed. On the other end of the scale large ones (#12 and #10 long shank) are required when the June bugs make their appearance.

Beetle-eating trout are generally soft risers, feeding daintily as if they know the insect can't get off the water. Leaders should be as long and fine as possible, consistent with the size and weight of the hook, and the strike to the rise should be only a gradual tightening of the line, much as in midge fishing.

The Quill-Back Beetle may be tied in a variety of sizes and shapes.

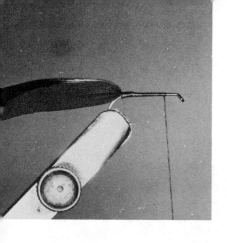

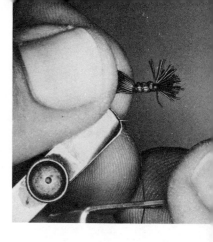

TYING THE QUILL-BACK BEETLE

1. Clamp a #14 fine wire hook in the vise and tie in black Nymo thread at bend. Cut one section each from a right and left black-dyed duck wing quill. Place quill sections back to back (glossy sides inside) and bind tips to hook at bend. Quill sections should stand on edge like wet fly wings. Spiral thread forward and half-hitch 1/8-inch behind eye.

2. Cut a small bunch of black-dyed deer body hair from hide. Bunch should be about 3/16 inch wide when flattened. Bind hair to hook behind eye and spiral thread in firm, spaced turns back to bend, where quill sections were tied in.

3. Maintaining firm tension, spiral thread forward over hair and half-hitch behind flared butts of hair. Trim butts close to hook as shown.

4. (Top view) Separate hair at bend into two equal bunches. Hold one bunch at right angle to hook and twist hair to form a rope-like strand. Then pull twisted hair forward and lay it alongside shank of hook. Tie off hair well behind eye as shown.

5. Twist the other bunch of hair, lay it along opposite side of hook and tie off. Half-hitch thread. Trim away excess hair, not too close to hook, allowing short, flared butts to remain.

6. Coat dull side of nearest quill section with vinyl cement and apply quill, with cement still tacky, over nearest half of beetle's back, moulding edge of quill around side. Bind quill to hook behind hair butts.

7. Repeat step 6 with other quill section, making sure the two sections overlap on back. Invert hook in vise and tie in three short strands of black Nymo thread for legs, crisscrossed as shown. Trim legs to size and apply a drop of vinyl cement to tips of legs to prevent fraying.

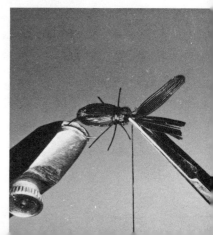

8. Return hook to normal position in vise. Overlap ends of quill sections and position them over trimmed hair butts. Tie down with two turns of thread behind eye and trim away excess quill as shown. Whip finish and apply head lacquer to exposed windings. A thin coating of vinyl cement over the quill back completes the pattern.

The Quill-Back Japanese Beetle

Popillia japonica, the Japanese beetle: the very mention of its name stirs wrath within the hearts of farmers and gardeners alike for this destructive little pest leaves its mark wherever it appears. Accidentally introduced into this country in 1916, there are few regions east of the Mississippi which have escaped its onslaught. Perhaps its most dramatic appearance was in the early 1940s when it made entrance into the Cumberland Valley of Pennsylvania. It took two keen observers, Charlie Fox and Vince Marinaro, to note its abundance along the lush meadow streams and to foresee its influence on the surface-feeding activities of trout. In the two decades to follow a unique chapter in the history of dry fly fishing was written, so bizarre that it may never be duplicated. The story has often been told but somehow the singularity of the epoch remains undiminished. To say that the trout became oriented to the little intruders from Asia is to force an unwarranted pun upon our readers, but in the literal sense it is also an understatement. The daily spectacle of trout rising steadily in the hottest part of the day to nonaquatic insects, and over a continuous span of two months, was an extravaganza not even Halford would have contemplated.

Eventually state and federal agencies were able to deal with the Japanese beetle in the areas of its most massive infestations. It is no longer found in the seething, crawling armies which abounded in the limestone spring meadows. Agriculturalists breathed a collective sigh of relief but fair-minded anglers were torn between two emotions. On the one hand they were sympathetic with those who suffered damage from the pests, knowing full well the floral destruction had to be stopped. At the same time there was a tinge of sadness that an insect so plentiful and so appealing to trout could not have been more

Completed Quill-Back Japanese Beetle

beneficial to man.

But despite the success in controlling Japanese beetles where they were most devastating, there are still fair numbers extant. Most rose-growers would agree that the report of their demise, like that of Mark Twain, was rather exaggerated. In any event, they fit into the roster of terrestrial insects properly deserving of imitation.

Our Japanese Beetle pattern is tied quill-back style, with coppery brown, folded wings and black thorax, with legs comprised of individual fibres teased out from the sides of the black quill section forming the thorax. The underbody is of black-dyed deer body hair tied in a bundle over the shank, separated at the rear into two bunches, each of which is twisted, brought along the side and tied off in front. The latter maneuver provides the ovoid shape of the insect's abdomen. The material itself supplies the buoyancy necessary in a good floater.

For a while I tried to imitate the dark metallic green underside of the natural by weaving strands of a peacock herl through the deer hair, but I'm convinced it wasn't worth the effort. The herl, fragile at best, not only rendered the pattern less durable but it absorbed water and hindered its floatability. The trout don't seem to mind the black underview of the pattern and they are the most severe critics a fly can have.

Duck wing quill feathers are easy to dye, and if pre-dyed brown quills (for the pattern's folded wings) are not easily obtainable it's a simple task to tint them the proper shade. Begin with a matched pair of white quill feathers and immerse them in a solution of two parts rust and one part brown household dyes until the desired shade is achieved. It's difficult to go wrong if the instructions on the dye packages are followed. As an alternative, the tinting may be accomplished by stroking the quill sections—or the whole feathers—with a colorfast brown, felt-tipped marking pen. In the latter method the color's permanence is assured by coating the quill with vinyl, as prescribed in the tying instructions.

Popillia japonica

1. Clamp a size #14 dry fly hook in the vise and tie in black Nymo thread at bend. Cut a section each from a matched pair of brown-dyed duck quill feathers and tie in by tips at bend, glossy sides facing each other. Spiral thread forward 2/3 length of shank and half-hitch.

2. Cut a thinnish bundle (about 3/16 inch wide when flattened) of black-dyed deer body hair and hold over shank with hair tips extending over quill sections. Bind hair to hook and spiral thread to rear around hair and hook. Half-hitch just forward of quill tie-in and spiral thread back to hair tie-in. Half-hitch and trim hair butts as shown.

3. Arrange hair at rear into two equal bunches and train each bunch upward and away from quill sections.

4. (Top view) Grasp hair of one bunch by tips and twist several times, forming a rope, then lay rope alongside hook in a curving arc and tie off at thorax position. Repeat with other bunch of hair on opposite side.

5. Trim tips of hair in shape shown.

6. Coat outside (dull side) of one quill section with vinyl cement and pull quill over one side of hair underbody, moulding quill over back and along side. Tie off quill at thorax position. Repeat on opposite side with other quill section. Trim off excess quill.

7. Cut a section of black-dyed duck quill a little wider than abdomen. Tie in over body at thorax position with glossy side down and tips extending over eye.

8. (Top view) With bodkin, separate three fibres from each side of black quill section and arrange as legs. Wind thread between and against base of legs to lock in position. Wind thread to eye and trim excess quill as shown. Coat dull side of black quill with vinyl and pull forward over thorax. Tie off at eye and trim excess. Whip-finish thread behind eye and lacquer tie-off. Trim legs to desired length and coat legs lightly with vinyl.

The Horse Fly

I make it a point to spend some time each fishing day seated on a rock, next to a strategic line of current, sampling the surface with a fine-meshed aquarium net. This doesn't tell me specifically what the trout are feeding upon, but it does demonstrate the nature and quantity of food available at a given time. I'm often amazed at the variety of both aquatic and terrestrial insects carried by the flow. During warm weather there are many drowned terrestrials floating flush in the film, usually unseen from the angler's position because they lack a silhouette against the surface. Among these are insects far from their natural habitats, like house flies, horse flies and many others which bear resemblance to these common pests.

I call this pattern a Horse Fly, but in sizes #10 down to #22 it is adaptable to many representations, from the robust bot flies to the little blue bottles. All share a squat appearance, with prominent eyes and wings folded flat over the back. The fly is dressed entirely with a single bunch of black-dyed deer body hair. The tying technique is both simple and unique. After cutting the hair from the hide the tips should be matched evenly, either by using a hair tamper or by withdrawing and replacing hairs until the desired effect is achieved. Then, using the hook as reference, the hair is measured from tips to tie-in point for an effective length of about three times the hook length, from eye to the outside of the bend. The hair is then tied in, butts forward, and bound as a bundle on top of the shank. Previously preparing the hook by winding the thread in cross turns along the shank provides a rough base which discourages the hair from rolling around the shank. The hair butts are trimmed off and the hair is folded forward, caught with a turn of thread behind the eye, then folded backward over a bodkin needle and caught again. Thus, the stout body, prominent head and eyes, and flat wings are all fashioned by strategically folding and binding the single hank of hair. If the hair has been accurately measured the tips (the wings) should extend a little beyond the outside of the bend. Three short lengths of hair, selected from the trimmed scraps, are then bound underneath to represent legs.

Because of the tension required to bind the hair securely, nylon thread of a gauge heavier than normally used for dry flies is recommended. When dressing the Horse Fly in the larger sizes deer body hair of rather coarse texture should be selected. As a point of reference, the bunch of hair for a size #14 should be about ¼ inch in width when flattened between the fingertips. Other sizes should be in proportion.

Owing to the hollow deer hair construction the Horse Fly is virtually unsinkable, particularly when a little line or fly floatant has been worked into it with the fingertips. However, this hair tends to be somewhat fragile and occasionally a trout's teeth will render the fly somewhat scraggly. This seems to be a fault more prevalent in the larger sizes because of the greater exposure. But "not to worry"; simply use your gut clippers to trim away the broken hairs and the fly will be ready to fish again—perhaps not as neat as when new, but equally effective. Besides, I've always felt that when a fly begins to take on a chewed-up appearance it's an indication that it has done an honest day's work. And the Horse Fly is so easy to tie that replenishing the box is hardly a chore.

Completed Horse Fly

TYING THE HORSE FLY

1. Clamp hook (size #14 shown) in vise and tie in black thread at a point about 1/3 shank length behind eye. Spiral thread in spaced turns back to bend, then forward again, creating a cross pattern. Half-hitch at tie-in point. Cut a bunch of black-dyed deer body hair and even the tips. The effective length of the hair, from tips to tie-in, should be three full hook lengths.

2. Hold hair on top of shank, butts forward, and bind to hook at tie-in point. Then spiral thread in firm, spaced turns around hair and shank, back to bend.

3. Without easing tension, wind thread forward in similar spacing and half-hitch at point of tie-in. Trim excess hair butts, as shown.

4. Grasp hair by tips and fold forward over hook. Catch with thread behind eye and half-hitch.

5. Place bodkin needle crossways on hair and fold hair back over needle, as shown. Holding hair in position over back with left hand, withdraw needle. Then throw a loop of thread over hair and draw tight. Half-hitch.

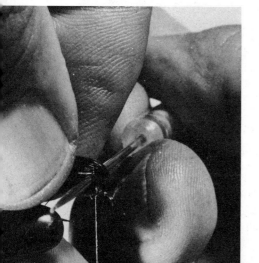

6. (Bottom view) For legs, select three short lengths of hair from trimmings and bind underneath body. Wind between legs to separate. Optionally, you may coat the legs with vinyl cement or acrylic lacquer and when half dry, bend leg joints with tweezers. Then whip finish head and apply a drop of head lacquer.

81

The Carpenter Ant

In the December 1962 issue of the *Pennsylvania Angler* I did a piece called "The Universal Ant," a general discussion of the role ants play in fly fishing. I mentioned a dry fly pattern called the Carpenter Ant, with which I had been experimenting for several years on both trout and panfish. It was a simple pattern, made entirely of black-dyed deer body hair, with gasters, or bulges, in the appropriate places and a few hairs bound back at the head to represent legs. Later I wrote an article specifically about the Carpenter Ant for the 1964 *Fishermen's Digest*, with illustrations detailing the dressing procedure.

It wasn't long afterwards that I was taken to task by a talented young fly tyer on the LeTort who reminded me that an ant's legs originate at its midriff, not its head. Actually, I had noticed this, too, but since the pattern had been intended as impressionistic I felt that the latter placement was probably more expedient. But my young friend had made a good point and I couldn't quarrel with his realistic approach, particularly on the LeTort, where such seemingly trivial matters are sometimes important.

The dressing shown here is that of the revised version of the Carpenter Ant, with pedal extremities emanating from its waist. I have been tying and fishing both versions for nearly twenty years and with it I have caught trout in just about every stream I have fished. I have heard from anglers all over the country that they are using it with success for western cutthroat in coastal streams, brown trout in Montana's spring creeks, brook trout in Maine, and southern bream in Arkansas. Our friend, Bob Runk, fished the pattern successfully to Irish brown trout.

Although it is primarily a hot weather pattern there have been several occasions when the Carpenter Ant worked wonders on opening day. Of course, those were the lucky times when weather and water conditions were just right for fishing dry in mid-April. During the hottest months it is a high-noon fly on bright days when terrestrial insects are most active and trout lie along grassy banks, waiting for whatever fare the currents will guide their way. To me, of all seasons, autumn is the time of the Carpenter Ant. The mountain streams are generally low, and they are possessed of a clearness unsurpassed at any other time of the angler's year. By early October the fallen leaves of the hardwoods begin to drift with the flow and build up at the tails of slow pools to form additional overhead cover for trout. The gaudy colors of the leaves seem to complement the prenuptial complexion of the trout; altogether, it is a time when nature's galleries are at their brilliant best.

Although the real Carpenter Ant is a large insect, warranting in its representation a hook of perhaps size #12, I use the pattern mainly in sizes #14 through #18, preferring the winged, fur-bodied ants in the really diminutive sizes since they are a bit easier to see on the water. If your eyes are extra keen and can follow the tiniest speck on the surface, by all means try the Carpenter Ant in sizes #22 and #24.

The pattern owes its buoyancy to the hollowness of deer body hair which, when compressed, traps air within the bulges. But the hollowness also contributes to the fragility of the hair; for this reason it is prudent to use eight or ten hairs for legs instead of nature's allotment of six. This will compensate for the inevitable loss of a leg or two to the sharp teeth of trout. As to the placement of the legs, it is perhaps more aesthetically satisfying to position them at the waist but frankly I haven't seen any improvement in effectiveness over the pattern's original version. When ants drift sodden in the surface film their legs are generally askew in an unpredictable posture and not in any definite arrangement as when they are crawling on land. So, take your choice and tie whichever version pleases you; I'm sure the trout won't care.

Carpenter ant

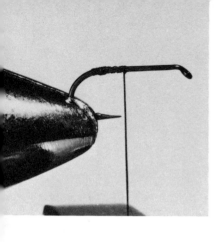

TYING THE CARPENTER ANT

1.   Clamp a dry fly hook (#16 shown) in vise and tie in black nylon nymph thread at bend. Spiral thread forward about 1/3 length of shank and half-hitch. Then cut a bundle of black-dyed deer body hair about twice as thick as a kitchen match.

2.   Hold hair in left hand over hook with tips pointing left and butts projecting slightly forward of half-hitched thread. Make a double loop of thread around hair and shank, then pull tight, causing butts to flare. Then tightly spiral thread in spaced turns back to bend. Half-hitch. Trim off flared hair butts.

3.   Wind thread forward in tight spirals, spacing the turns equally and crossing the already wound thread in an "X" pattern. Half-hitch over trimmed hair butts. Then pull the bunch of free hair forward, over the shank, and stroke toward tips to remove any slack in individual hairs. Holding hair over shank with right hand, with left make a loop around hair and hook, then pull tight.

4.   (Top view) To represent waist, wind thread forward tightly around hair, and shank for about four close turns. Pull back four or five hairs on each side to represent legs, then continue waist ahead of legs with four more close turns.

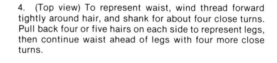

5.   Trim legs to desired length. With left hand lift remaining bunch of hair while winding thread forward, around shank only, to about 1/2 the distance to eye.

6.   Form small gaster by holding hair over shank, throwing a loop of thread around hair and hook, then pulling thread tight. Again, lift hair and wind thread forward around shank to a point just behind eye of hook.

7.   Repeat previous step to form another bulge representing head. Then trim away excess hair as shown and whip finish thread at eye. Remove thread and apply head lacquer to whip finish.

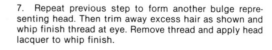

8.   Matching the hatch. Completed Carpenter Ant below; original version above.

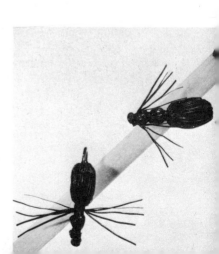

An Upwing Ant

The role ants play in the fly fisher's scheme has only been fully appreciated in the past few decades. True, shortly after the turn of the century Halford wrote that winged ants were sometimes taken by trout (pattern number 28 of his celebrated series of dry flies was assigned to their representation) but his treatment of ants was more an acknowledgment of their occasional presence on trout water than a detailed study. Not that Halford could be faulted for this; in his development of the dry fly the entire concept was so new and revolutionary that primary attention was focused on representing the more obvious Ephemeroptera. But fly fishermen have now had the benefit of three-quarters of a century's continuing refinement of the floating fly, fostered by talented and thoughtful anglers, and it was inevitable that the lowly ant would eventually get its due.

Although no stage in the life cycle of ants is aquatic, they manage to present themselves to trout in several ways. Wingless worker ants of all sizes fall into the water in random fashion, shaken from their perches by wind or swollen streams. They are carried by the current in or just under the surface film. Numerically, like most terrestrial insects, the wingless ants may appear rather insignificant as trout fare at any given time. However, they are likely to be present, albeit in limited numbers, over most of the season, and trout get to know them well. On the other hand, winged ants—the mating forms —appear only at certain times during summer and fall but they sometimes occur in such numbers near streams that their presence on the water rivals heavy falls of mayfly spinners. Since the males always die after mating, they make up the preponderance of winged ants on the water. The females return to the earth, where they rid themselves of their wings and either begin small colonies of their own or enter established colonies to lay their eggs.

Mating swarms appear to occur simultaneously over wide areas. On a hot summer night several years ago I was tying flies at my desk at home, in preparation for a weekend fishing trip two or three days hence. As I worked I suddenly became aware that two little winged ants— tiny enough to have crawled through the fine-meshed window screen—were scurrying along my vise. Were they trying to tell me something? Evidently they were because on the following Saturday, at a stream fully 140 miles from home, winged ants seemed to be everywhere and they inspired much of the feeding activity of that day.

There are times when winged ants float with their wings in an upright position totally unlike the prone, flush-floating attitude commonly ascribed to these insects on the water. In fact, with wings aloft their posture is nearly identical to that of drifting mayfly duns, for which I'm certain they are often mistaken, particularly from a distance. But despite the similarity in wing profile, there are too many anatomical dissimilarities between the two insects to render a mayfly representation consistently successful when ants are on the water—or vice-versa.

The Upwing Ant is my own interpretation of the little Hymenopterans in the sail-like attitude and it has become a valuable addition to my dry fly kit. It's not an everyday fly but on those occasions when its use was indicated it has produced admirably. Too, the prominent wings make it easier to see on the water than the flat-floating types and to me that's a plus.

The pattern is basically pure ant: prominent gasters of dubbed fur both fore and aft with a slim waist between. Ants' wings are shaped much like those of mayflies and in the pattern they are cut to configuration from hen hackles, using scissors, a wing cutter, or preferably, the ingenious nail clipper method originated by Poul Jorgensen. A single hackle is wound sparsely at the waist and trimmed underneath, preserving the view of the tall wings and at the same time insuring the low-floating characteristic of the natural. Useful sizes are #18 through #22. It has been my experience that the larger ants are more prevalent in autumn.

Both black and red ants should be represented. Although the photographs show the dressing for the black ant, the red Upwing Ant is tied similarly, with the following variation in materials:

Thread: Brown Herb Howard's 6/0, prewaxed
Dubbing: Reddish-brown kapok, fur or synthetic
Wings: Cut and shaped from rusty dun hen hackles
Hackle: Brown

1. Tie in fine, black thread at bend of a dry fly hook and wax about 2 inches of thread next to shank. Apply a moderately thin dubbing of black fur, kapok, or synthetic. Build up abdominal gaster with dubbing as shown and wind bare thread forward to form thin waist.

2. For wings, select two pale dun hen hackles and cut to shape with wing cutter, scissors, or nail clippers. Length of wings should be equal to overall length of hook. Hold wings together and bend stems forward with tweezers.

3. Tie wings in place at fore end of waist by binding bent stems on top of shank. Trim excess stems and apply a drop of cement at base of wings. Then select a web-free black hackle with barbs about as long as 1½ times hook gap and tie in behind wings.

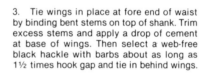

4. Wind hackle over waist with two turns and tie off in front of wings. Trim waste hackle tip.

5. Apply a little more black dubbing to waxed thread and build smaller gaster in front of wings, as shown. Finally, whip finish, apply head lacquer and trim an inverted "V" from underside of hackle.

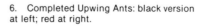

6. Completed Upwing Ants: black version at left; red at right.

85

The Spent Black Ant

There are certain fly patterns that become identified with specific streams because they are particularly effective on those waters. Any mention of beetles and jassids almost automatically brings to mind the LeTort and when I think of Penn's Creek, stonefly nymphs are suggested. I learned about the importance of ants on Spring Creek, particularly at Fisherman's Paradise, where ant patterns have earned an exalted rank.

During the early days of the Paradise there was a refreshment stand outside the main gate where anglers could buy sandwiches, soft drinks, and items of fishing gear—particularly flies. The stock of fly patterns was generally excellent but most in evidence were boxes of hard ants, tied wet-fly in black, brown, and red and in a variety of sizes.

There was good reason for the ample supply of ant patterns. In those days the Paradise regulations permitted the killing of two trout of prescribed minimum size and it was not unusual to see a happy angler trudging along the path from the woods, carrying an arm-long brown trout to the checking station. Naturally, a trout of trophy size attracts a lot of attention and soon the lucky angler resembled the Pied Piper, with an accumulating crowd behind him. Eventually, someone would ask the obvious question, to which the answer would invariably be, ''Black Ant . . . size #16.'' That would trigger a small stampede to the refreshment stand and soon the ant bin would be empty, much to the chagrin of stragglers who were late in getting the word. I've often thought that an enterprising fly tyer could have set up shop along the road next to the Paradise and made a small fortune tying flies to order. There were that many anglers who would have paid a king's ransom for *the fly*.

In the early 1950s it was our pleasure to introduce Paul Young to Pennsylvania trout fishing, and on our way north we stopped at the Paradise for a few hours. Large browns were surface-feeding on tiny insects. Paul, fascinated, chose to watch, wondering how trout of that heft could afford to expend the energy to rise for such minute fare. Large trout were not strangers to the Michigan angler but on his home streams their capture generally meant fishing after dark with large flies.

Just above the upper bridge was a large willow tree with an arched branch touching the water, forming a shaded canopy. The pull of the current against the trailing branch would cause it to flex, lift an inch above the surface, and dip down again in a rhythmic, repetitive sequence. Lying just behind the branch was a fine trout which I chose to ignore because I thought he was in an impossible position. But Mr. Young had spotted the trout, too, and he suggested that the footbridge would give him a fine vantage point for his movie camera if I would try for the trout.

Now I was somewhat in awe of fishing with one of America's great fly fishermen and I felt like a piano student performing for Arthur Rubenstein. But I didn't know how to decline gracefully, so I nervously tied on a size #22 Cinnamon Ant, tied spent with a fur body. I punched a cast under the canopy, knowing full well that the leader or fly would run afoul of the trailing branch. But instead, miraculously, the branch lifted clear at precisely the right moment and the fly floated under, directly into the jaws of the waiting trout. A gleeful Paul Young recorded the action on 16 mm film, from the cast to the netting of the fish, and I feigned nonchalance, as if this were an everyday happening. I should have retired then and there because I'll never make a luckier cast.

I've had outstanding fishing on many streams with hair carpenter ants and the little fur-bodied ants, both upwing and spent, but some of the Paradise experiences stand uppermost in memory. We were there during a mating flight of tiny winged ants when the stream was virtually blanketed with their spent forms for several hours. I was fishing the project's upstream water with a little black spent ant and took trout after trout along the pumphouse wall. They were big, high-jumping browns that took the fly with the most imperceptible of rise forms.

My own version of the fur-bodied spent ant is quite like the now standard patterns, except for the wings. Instead of a hackle wound at the waist and bunched or clipped top and bottom, I use two small bunches of hackle barbules mixed—with tips of one bunch matched to the butts of the other to achieve uniform density overall—then separated and flattened, following which they are trimmed to size. I have been using this type of spent wings for several years with good results. It allows me to use the large (and otherwise often useless) hackles from necks, preserving my small hackles, the supply of which is growing short these days.

The illustrations show the dressing of the Spent Black Ant. The Spent Cinnamon Ant is tied identically with brown tying thread, reddish-brown body dubbing, and pale ginger or dark cream hackle barbules.

Left: Black Spent Ant
Right: Cinnamon Spent Ant

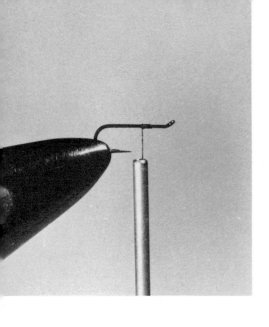

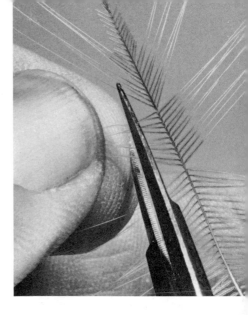

TYING A SPENT BLACK ANT

1. Clamp a dry fly hook in vise (best sizes are #18 to #24) and tie in fine, black tying thread just forward of the center of shank.

2. Select a large, medium dun tackle and stroke the center rib from the tip downward to splay the barbules at right angles. Cut a bunch of ten to twelve barbules from one side of hackle and place, tips down, in hair packer. Then cut a corresponding bunch from other side of hackle and place in packer, butts down. Withdraw all barbules as a single bunch and roll between fingertips to mix.

3. Bind bunch of barbules to top of shank with figure-eight turns and cut off tips to proper wing length. Then bring thread up through barbules on near side, over shank and through barbs on far side. This separates and spreads the barbules.

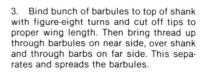

4. Make a turn of thread around shank behind wing. Then bring thread laterally under base of far wing, over shank in front, under base of near wing and over shank behind wings. This maneuver flattens the wings. Then wind thread to bend.

5. Wax a short length of the thread next to the hook and apply a dubbing of fine, black fur, or kapok. Wind dubbing to form ball-like abdominal gaster. Then wind thread to three turns in front of wings, leaving narrow waist.

6. Dub a bit more fur on thread and wind a smaller ball (the pedicel) in front of wings. Whip finish at eye and cut thread. Apply lacquer to head and windings at base of wings. Finally, trim ends of wings round.

The Quill-Back Cricket

Something about the hopping insects seems to fascinate and excite trout, causing them to throw off their usual instincts of caution. Like grasshoppers, crickets offer a substantial mouthful to a waiting fish, and with their highly developed hind legs, they make a commotion on the water that unmistakably announces their presence.

No part of the cricket's life cycle is aquatic; yet, grassy banks along streams often abound in cricket life and enough of these cheerful insects get into the water to attract the attention of the trout. The common field cricket, which the Quill-Back Cricket represents, is especially plentiful along the limestone meadow streams.

The approach to a dry fly representing the cricket is far different from that of the Ephemerids, for unlike the mayflies, the cricket floats low, riding flush in the water's surface film. This attitude negates conventional hackling, and flotation of the fly must instead be achieved by a buoyant body material. The use of hollow deer hair, tied longitudinally on the hook and tightly segmented with thread to trap air pockets, serves perfectly.

Some years ago I tied and used a cricket made almost entirely of deer body hair and a highly successful pattern it was. But trout have sharp teeth and the all-hair cricket often became chewed up sooner than the painstaking tying effort warranted. The tie was modified several times before we hit upon the idea of using a section of vinyl-coated goose quill over the back to protect the deer hair. The tough vinyl coating not only prevents breaking up of the delicate material but it helps to maintain the body shape. The Quill-Back Cricket is not only durable and a good floater, but it attracts big trout.

The Fish-For-Fun Paradise water on Spring Creek is an ideal testing ground for terrestrial patterns and it was here that the Q-B Cricket had an impressive initiation on a June afternoon some years ago. It was a hot day and my wife and I had hiked to the shaded upper end of the project water to get out of the sun. On the opposite side of a long pool there was a heavy rise in a little slack-water bay, snug against the road embankment. The trout was in a difficult spot to reach. The back cast had to be thrown through a narrow opening in the trees and the forward cast sent high and stopped over the mark, creating enough slack to allow the fly to float for a few seconds before drag took over.

My first two casts were short of the mark, I suppose mainly because I was a little timid about hanging up in the trees behind me. Finally when a cast landed just right, a pointed snout parted the surface and took the Cricket. The big trout never jumped but he tore up and down the pool several times, occasionally thrashing at the surface, before the constant rod pressure turned his head. Eventually, a magnificent specimen of brown trout was netted, a male of 23 inches with a hooked lower jaw.

Although the illustrations show the tying procedure for a black Q-B Cricket, a brown pattern may be dressed by substituting reddish-brown deer body hair for the body, dyed brown duck quill for the back and brown tying thread. It's a good idea to have both black and brown patterns on hand.

As an alternative, realistic forelegs may be dressed by substituting two goose quill fibres of correct color for Nymo. After trimming the fibres to length, coat with thin vinyl cement or acrylic lacquer and when nearly dry, bend leg joints with tweezers.

Tradition has it that a cricket on the hearth is a good omen of luck. So, too, is a supply of Crickets in the flybox.

Cricket

TYING THE
QUILL-BACK CRICKET

1. Place a size #14 long shank hook in vise and tie in size A black Nymo thread at bend. Allow about a 4-inch end of thread to hang free as shown and spiral spool end of thread forward to eye. Cut off thread hanging at bend and lay aside for later use.

2. For antennae select two straight black bear hairs and tie in just behind eye. Half-hitch. Antennae should be about twice the length of hook shank.

3. Cut a medium-thick bunch of deer body hair (dyed black) from the hide and hold in left hand with butts extending over eye. Take a loose turn of thread around hair and lower hair to hook. Take up slack in thread, bring thread under hook and over hair and gradually pull thread tight, causing hair butts to flare. Half-hitch. (Initial loop of thread around hair keeps hair on top of hook.)

4. Maintaining position of hair with left hand, spiral thread tightly around hair, work toward bend of hook. Spirals should be spaced about 1/8 inch apart.

5. Half-hitch thread at bend of hook. Body should have three or four segments with hair flaring both front and back.

6. Carefully trim hair in front to a ball-shaped head. Avoid cutting antennae. Holding thread out of the way, trim hair in back to a point. Trimming may be easier if hook is removed from vise.

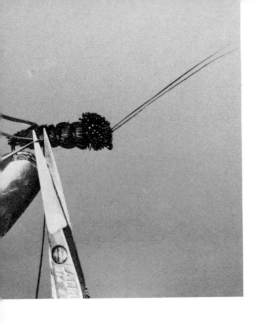

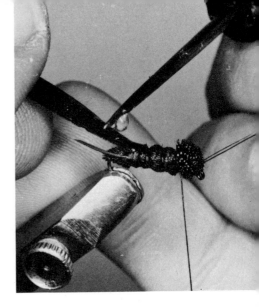

7. For tails select two dark condor quill fibres and tie in against sides of body at rear winding. Fold back butt of each quill fibre and take two turns of thread over fold, locking tails in place. Trim away excess butts as shown.

8. For quill back cut a section of dyed black goose primary, about 3/16 inch wide. Tie thin end flat over tail windings with shiny side down so that butt end of quill section extends back over rear of hook. Spiral thread forward and half-hitch behind head. With bodkin point, spread a drop of thin vinyl cement on top of quill section. While still tacky, fold quill forward and press against back. Tie off behind head with two turns.

9. Trim away excess quill section snug against windings.

10. Tie in two condor quill fibres to represent kicker legs at sides of body behind head. Tips should extend back almost to tips of tails. Fold back butts of condor quill and wind over fold as in step 7. Trim away excess. (Note: If condor quill is not available the tails and kicker legs may be made of black goose quill fibres, taken from the short side of the primary.)

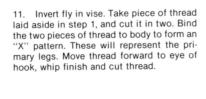

11. Invert fly in vise. Take piece of thread laid aside in step 1, and cut it in two. Bind the two pieces of thread to body to form an "X" pattern. These will represent the primary legs. Move thread forward to eye of hook, whip finish and cut thread.

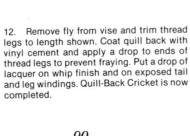

12. Remove fly from vise and trim thread legs to length shown. Coat quill back with vinyl cement and apply a drop to ends of thread legs to prevent fraying. Put a drop of lacquer on whip finish and on exposed tail and leg windings. Quill-Back Cricket is now completed.

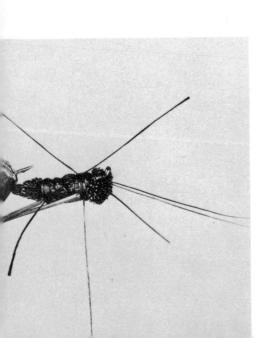

The Single-Hank 'Hopper

There is a peculiar fascination in 'hopper fishing, especially on the meadow streams. Here the angler must stalk his prey like a bow hunter, often creeping along on hands and knees in the tall grass because the trout are shy and concealment is important. The quarry is frequently found underneath the cover of overhanging grass, or along a watercress bed at the stream's edge, waiting for whatever fare the current brings him. The cast should be made from a crouch—or even from a sitting position—for to stand erect on the bank risks scaring the trout and spoiling the angler's chance for success.

Most veteran 'hopper fishermen will tell you that trout prefer the yellow-bodied short-horned grasshoppers over the green varieties, which include the katydid. This has been my experience, too, with a few exceptions, and they present tempting morsels for birds and animals as well as fish.

There are many 'hopper patterns around today but those made of deer hair are the most trouble-free. A small amount of silicone paste worked into the hair will keep a 'hopper of this type floating indefinitely. I've always felt that many commercially available patterns, tied on size #8 or #10 hooks, are oversized for most eastern fishing. I could be quite happy with nothing but #14s in my 'hopper compartment, but I do carry a few #16's and #18's for early summer. Of course, the few grasshoppers still around by late fall are quite large and justify larger patterns.

The Single-Hank 'Hopper was so designated because, except for the kicker legs, it is made from a single hank of hair. The hair is natural deer body hair, of medium shade with speckled tips, dyed yellow. When dyed, the lighter shanks of the hair take on a yellowish cast while the darker tips remain brownish. Tied as prescribed, the doubled body and head of the fly are distinctly yellow, while the wings are somewhat darker. The kicker legs are single quill fibres from a goose quill feather dyed rust and are taken from the short side of the feather.

I have caught many good trout on the S-H 'Hopper but one I remember most vividly was one I didn't quite catch. We were fishing a rather large stream on a hot August afternoon and doing surprisingly well, considering the intensity of the blazing sun. I had fished up through a deep pool to an island, around which my wife, Marion, was fishing. She told me she had earlier seen what appeared to be a large brown trout wallowing in a shallow pocket next to the high bank. Curious, I waded over to midstream, where I could watch the pocket from a discreet distance. The pocket was formed by an indentation in the bank, and the opening was blocked by a half-submerged log. The current between me and the pocket was swift and there didn't appear to be any way one could make a fly sit in that pocket long enough for the trout to see it, much less take it.

Common sense told me to move on and fish elsewhere but the blind rationale of the fly fisher prevailed and I decided to make "just one cast." I threw high and hard toward the bank, checked the cast abruptly and, marvel of marvels, the 'hopper dropped into the pocket with loose leader to spare. The fly sat there an eternal two seconds when a pointed snout parted the surface and took it. What happened then is mostly a blur in my recollection but I remember applying all the pressure I dared, to keep his head up, and, miraculously, he slithered *over* the log and into the main flow. Helped by the current, the trout bolted downstream to the pool below and I finally caught up with him there. Eventually, the big tail began to fan feebly above the surface and I knew the struggle would shortly be ended. As I drew him over the outstretched net I was mesmerized by his big spots, the gold-plated gill covers and flaming crimson adipose fin. Suddenly I was aware that the rod pressure had relaxed and the big trout sank slowly, turned, and swam off into deep water. The hold of the hook had simply come undone!

Maybe it's best I didn't land that trout. If he really were as big as I thought, no one would have believed me—except my wife. But that's the way it is with 'hopper fishing; there's nothing *average* about it.

Completed Single-Hank 'Hopper

TYING THE
SINGLE-HANK 'HOPPER

1. Insert a size #14 dry fly hook in vise and tie in yellow nymph thread behind eye. Wind thread to bend, then spiral it back to point of tie-in. Cut a smallish bunch (when twisted, about twice the diameter of a kitchen match) of yellow-dyed deer body hair and match the tips evenly. As shown, measure the hair to about 3½ times the length of the shank. This is the effective wing length.

2. Bind hair (tips toward bend) on top of shank behind eye. Hold hair in bundle over shank and spiral thread around hair and shank to bend in firm, spaced turns. Then trim excess hair butts in front, as shown.

3. Arrange hair extending over bend into a tight bundle and fold forward over underbody. Spiral thread forward around doubled body, again in tight, spaced turns to just behind eye.

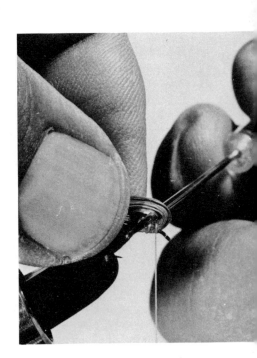

4. Lay bodkin needle over hair at tie-in windings. Fold hair up and over needle. Hold with left hand in this position and remove needle.

5. Take two or three turns of thread around hair and hook, forming head and setting wings in position.

6. For kicker legs, select two fibres from the short side of a goose quill feather, dyed rust. Place along either side of body and secure with two turns behind head. Then bend butts backwards and wind over folded portion to lock in place. Trim excess butts. Finally, whip finish thread behind eye and apply head lacquer.

The Flexi-Inchworm

There is a time in the fly fisher's season when his thoughts turn to worm fishing, but with a twist. It's not the type of worm angling many veterans practice a month earlier with such artistry and deadly precision. Rather, it fits the mold of conventional dry fly fishing to surface-feeding trout in almost every respect except pattern and delivery. In late spring and early summer, along streams with broad-leaved shade trees on their banks, the inchworms appear, dangling from nearly invisible filaments to drive trout crazy. Find a hardwood tree overhanging the water during inchworm time and you'll most likely find several good trout beneath it, daring the succulent larvae to touch the surface.

Inchworms—or measuring worms, as they are often called—are the larvae of the Geometrid moths (also called Geometer moths by some authorities).

In the early 1950s I began tying and fishing an inchworm pattern dressed with a single bunch of deer body hair bound as a slim, cylindrical bundle on a long-shanked hook. The pattern was very successful but I've since changed my mind about the long-shank requirement and it is now dressed on a hook of regular shank with a body extension about equal to the shank length. The extra extension exploits the flexibility of the deer hair, permitting it to be bent in a curve to the right or left and upward or downward. This more nearly simulates the posture of the natural inchworms, which seldom float along ruler-straight.

Gerald Almy, in his excellent new book *Tying and Fishing Terrestrials*, stresses the audible impact made by land insects alighting on the water as a factor attractive to trout. Few terrestrial insects are endowed by nature with the delicate structure and bearing of the Ephemeropterans. Generally heavy-bodied and lacking in air resistance, their entry to the water is more collision than landing and trout become attuned to this dinner signal, often moving a considerable distance to intercept their hapless prey. In addition to the audible aspect, anything striking the water with force creates a geometric, star-shaped burst on the mirrorlike underside of the surface film, visible a long way under water, and probably appearing as a brilliant flash of light to a trout.

Dragging a dry fly upstream is not usually acceptable practice, but with inchworms it's different. The naturals often descend to the water with their strand of filament

The Flexi-Inchworm bends to zig to the right or zag to the left.

angling downstream against the pull of the current. They are also able to retrieve themselves, as if being reeled in from above, and when this occurs they scoot upstream on the surface before becoming airborne. I've found that simulating this maneuver can be an effective way to fish pocket water. Using a short line and high rod, I like to cast to the downstream end of a likely pocket and drag the artificial upstream with little or no leader touching the surface. It's not necessary to use fine leaders for this type of fishing; in fact, it's advisable to use tippets of heavier gauge than normal because the rises are often explosive.

The Flexi-Inchworm is an improved version of the original pattern. It lends itself both to conventional upstream work and pocket skittering because it is virtually unsinkable. Almost any shade of dyed green deer body hair will do but my personal favorite is pale, whitish-green. It not only matches many of the naturals but it is extremely visible under the shaded situations where one normally fishes inchworms.

Hook: #14 or #16, regular shank
Thread: Pale green Monocord or nymph thread
Body: Deer body hair dyed pale green

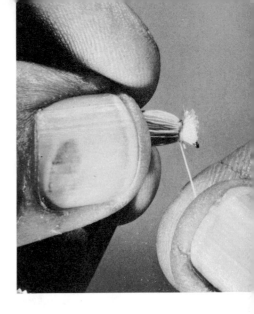

TYING THE FLEXI-INCHWORM

1. Tie in waxed thread behind eye of hook and wrap shank in spaced turns back to bend. Then reverse directions and wrap to beginning point. Half-hitch. Cut a bunch of dyed deer body hair about as thick as a pencil. Stroke out short hairs and fuzz.

2. Hold hair in a bundle on shank and bind to hook just behind eye, allowing about 1/8 inch of butts to project in front.

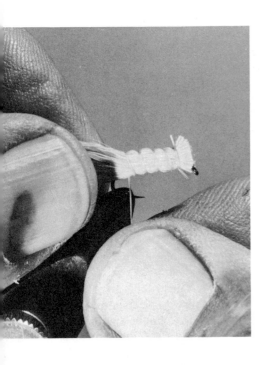

3. Holding hair in place with left hand, spiral thread in firm, spaced turns toward bend. Slide left hand to rear as winding progresses, always maintaining position of hair on shank.

4. When you reach the bend, continue to wrap hair in a free extension for a distance about equal to the portion already bound to shank. Make two extra turns at rearmost winding.

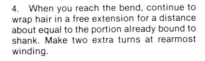

5. Then wind thread forward in similar spacing to eye. Whip finish, as shown.

6. Trim off excess hair at rear and finish-trim to a rounded profile. Trim hair in front to a neat head and apply black lacquer (as shown) to head and finish windings. Then apply clear lacquer to extra winds at rear.

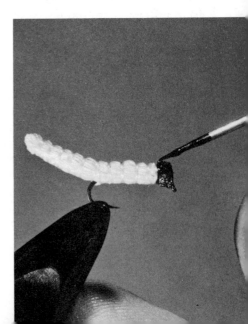

The Little Orange Mayfly

It's a . . . well, you would hardly call it a streamer fly in the usual sense, it's more like a . . . come to think of it, it's not quite like an ordinary wet fly, either. Nor is it a nymph. But whatever it is, it's a unique fly and there have been times when it has produced some mighty unusual results.

My first exposure to the pattern was three years ago, on a hot August afternoon when Hoagy Carmichael and I were tying flies for the evening's fishing. After we had dressed a modest supply of the essentials, Hoagy announced that he would show me a pattern I'd never seen, one that was often effective on his home Battenkill water in the fall. He then tied two specimens, on long-shanked, size #10 hooks, and deposited one in my flybox. It was an interesting fly with an orange body ribbed with a palmer-wound ginger hackle, trimmed to a mere stubble, and finished with a down wing and throat of wood duck flank fibres. I speculated that its somewhat gaudy coloration made it conspicuous in murky water following fall rains and during high water in spring. I hadn't anticipated what was to follow the next day—far from the Battenkill River in gin-clear midsummer water.

Four of us had packed our gear in the station wagon and had driven over to a favorite stretch of stream. When we arrived the air temperature was in the 90s and it seemed almost too hot to get into waders. But, don them we did and when we surveyed the stream from the bank and found nary a trout showing we decided to laze in the shade of the evergreens until things began to happen.

But not Hoagy.

After a few minutes of inactivity he lit his briar, tucked his rod under his arm, and waded to the head of the pool just below us. Naturally, the three of us on the bank directed a verbal barrage at him but the friendly insults stopped abruptly when his rod bent into an arc and his line began moving downstream. Eventually, he landed a magnificent male brook trout and in answer to the obvious question, he shouted back through a sheepish grin, "On a Little Orange Mayfly!"

Still unconvinced that it was anything but a fluke, we chided Hoagy about the dimwittedness of brook trout in general (which we didn't really believe) and of his catch, in particular. Whereupon he waded upstream and began to work back along our bank, catching good brown trout from under our very noses with alarming regularity. Needless to say, we lost little time getting into the water to try to emulate Hoagy's performance.

We have since found that trout don't *always* respond to the magic of the Little Orange Mayfly; that's simply too much to ask of any pattern. But besides the obvious occasions of high water, both early and late in the season, the pattern has produced surprising results under the most unlikely conditions.

There are several alternatives in materials that may be used to dress the Little Orange Mayfly. To add a little weight to the fly, use fine copper wire, obtainable in hobby or electronics shops, wound along the length of the shank. For extremely heavy water, lead wire may be used. Of course, the fly may be dressed without additional weight if desired. The body may be of orange floss, preferably heavy, or of yarn. If floss of medium weight is used, doubling the strand will furnish the requisite bulk. Although fibres from a wood duck flank feather are indicated for the wing and throat, similar fibres from teal or mallard should work equally well.

Hoagy Carmichael modestly disclaims credit for the origination of the Little Orange Mayfly but its appellation is distinctly his. You may fit it into any category you choose—wet fly, streamer or whatever—but it seems to do its best work when manipulated in short strokes like a streamer fly.

Completed Little Orange Mayfly

95

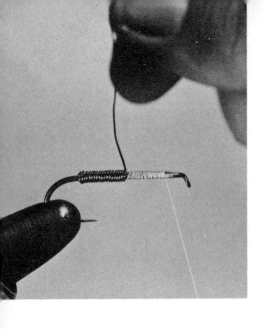

TYING THE LITTLE ORANGE MAYFLY

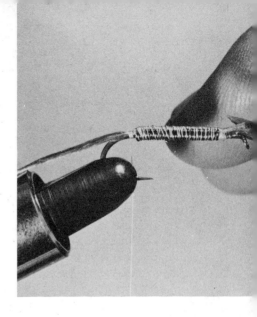

1. Clamp a size #10, 2X or 3X long shank hook in vise and bind yellow tying thread to shank behind eye. Tie in a 5-inch strand of fine copper wire and bind along shank to bend. Then return thread to head position. Grasp the free end of the wire and wind in close turns around shank to a point behind eye, leaving ample space for head. Tie off and trim excess wire.

2. Lay a length of orange floss (or yarn) on top of underbody, with one end overlapping eye. Bind with spiral turns back to bend, beyond underbody. Trim excess floss at head, as shown.

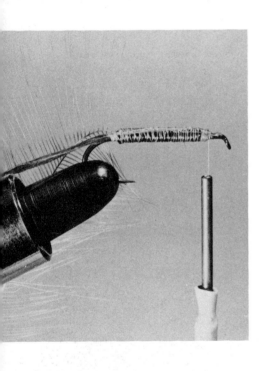

3. Select a large cream or light ginger hackle and splay the barbules by stroking downward along center stem. Tie in hackle by its tip behind underbody and spiral thread forward to head.

4. Wind floss to form tapered, medium-heavy body and tie off at head. Trim off excess floss. Then wind hackle forward in spaced turns and tie off at head. Trim waste hackle stem.

5. Trim hackle uniformly to a length of about 1/8 inch. For wing, bunch the fibres of the tip of a wood duck flank feather and tie in as shown. Tips of wing should not extend beyond outside of bend.

6. After trimming off excess wing butts, tie in a throat of wood duck fibres as shown. The throat should be considerably shorter than wing. Then remove waste fibres, build a neat head with thread, and whip finish. Lacquer head.